Locating and Correcting Reading Difficulties

Second Edition

ELDON E. EKWALL
University of Texas at El Paso

CHARLES E. MERRILL PUBLISHING COMPANY
A Bell & Howell Company
Columbus, Ohio

Published by
CHARLES E. MERRILL PUBLISHING COMPANY
A Bell & Howell Company
Columbus, Ohio 43216

This book was set in Times Roman.
The production editor was Jan Hall.
The cover was designed by Will Chenoweth.

International Standard Book Number: 0–675–08560–8
Library of Congress Catalog Card Number: 76–9885
5 6 7 8 9—82 81 80 79

Printed in the United States of America

TO
Jack Egan

Preface

The second edition of this book, as was the first, is designed to give busy reading teachers and students of reading concrete methods of locating and correcting reading difficulties. It can be used in developmental, corrective, and remedial situations. Although the basic format remains the same, the second edition contains a new section on contractions, more ideas and activities, and a list of basic sight words in Appendix H.

You should first turn to the section entitled "How to Use this Book." There you will find an explanation of format, which is simple to use and which will acquaint you with the multitude of ideas about teaching and correcting various reading abilities. You will note that in each category there is a short explanation of how to recognize problems with reading skills, a brief discussion of pertinent information on the problems, and specific recommendations on how to correct these difficulties. In some areas, you will also find games and activities to help strengthen reading abilities.

All of the ideas used in this book have been tried and proven successful, and the ideas contained in the first edition have proven successful by many more thousands of teachers. You should, however, remember that what works well with one student may not be appropriate with another. Furthermore, ideas that are suitable for one grade level may be unsuitable for another.

As with the first edition, this book is not designed to present the theory and philosophy of reading nor is it designed to take the place of a good reading methods course. It will, however, supplement teachers and students with concrete procedures which can be used in the classroom.

Throughout the book *he* will refer to a disabled reader. Since many studies have shown that more boys than girls are disabled in reading, it seems more appropriate to refer to such a reader as being male. No sex discrimination is intended.

Table of Contents

How to Use this Book

Read the "Definition of Terms" to be sure you are familiar with all of them before you begin to read the text. Then read the "Reading Diagnosis Sheet," (p. 5), which lists twenty-eight reading abilities and/or related abilities. Each section has the following organization. First an explanation is given for recognizing the difficulty with the ability listed. Then a discussion is presented to explain any pertinent information which is necessary for understanding or beginning to diagnose the problem. Specific recommendations for correcting any weaknesses in each of the abilities follow the discussion. Finally, under some sections, there is a list of games and exercises to help correct these difficulties. In most cases you could not, or would not, be able to attempt everything listed as a recommendation; however, you can choose the techniques which seem most appropriate for your situation.

After looking over the reading diagnosis sheet, read the entire book from beginning to end to insure familiarity with the contents. Having become familiar with the text, you should reproduce copies of the sheet in order to have a record for each member of the class; or if you are interested in diagnosing the difficulties of only one person, use the sheet found in the book.

Locating certain reading difficulties will be facilitated if you use the code for marking oral diagnosis which is listed in Appendix E. This code will enable you to find exactly what type of mistakes a student makes in his reading. With a little practice you will become adept at marking certain mistakes the pupils make in their oral reading. You will, of course, need a copy to mark as the pupil reads from his copy. You will find it also useful in rechecking a student's reading to discover if there is progress toward overcoming his earlier difficulties.

The reading diagnosis sheet is constructed to give you an opportunity to check each of the twenty-seven abilities listed three times during the year. The time period between checks will depend upon the intensity of the help or the normal teaching program. It could be as often as once a month or once during each semester of the school year. You should attempt to locate student difficulties as early in the year as possible. The "Recognized By" section of each skill will be helpful in determining whether certain skills are deficient. After determining which abilities are weak, tally the total number of students who are weak in each area and base your reading instruction on those areas in which the class as a whole is weakest. Then turn to the "Recommendations" and the "Games and Exercises" sections to use the suggestions given there.

The checklist does not categorize reading difficulties by the severity of the problem. You should be aware, however, that some of the items listed are of a more serious nature than others. Each discussion section explains how to determine whether the difficulty needs treatment, or whether it is only a symptom of a more serious problem. For example, word-by-word reading, improper phrasing, and repetitions usually are symptoms of more serious problems, such as difficulty in comprehension and/or word analysis or word recognition. In this situation, treatment for these larger problems probably would cause the symptoms of word-by-word reading, improper phrasing, and repetition to disappear automatically. You should read each discussion section carefully to insure adequate diagnosis and determine the proper improvement procedure.

Sometimes a particular suggestion will be appropriate with a younger child but will be inappropriate for an older student. The author has not listed various suggestions as appropriate for certain grades or age levels. You will need to exercise your own judgment based upon the severity of the problem, and the age and attitude of the child. The author has, however, made note that some problems are beyond the beginning reading stage.

Definition of Terms

Affix. A term meaning *to fasten,* usually applied to suffixes and prefixes collectively.

Basal reader. A reading book designed for a specific grade level. These usually contain material designed to enhance specific skills, such as word attack, vocabulary, and comprehension.

Basic sight word. These are words that are used many times over in the reading material written for both children and adults. One of the most common basic sight vocabulary lists is the *Dolch Basic Sight Vocabulary,** which contains no nouns. Other lists often contain some nouns. In Appendix H you will find the Corrective Reading System (CRS) *Basic Sight Word List* compiled by the author.

Blend. Combinations of two or three letters blended together into sounds while retaining the sounds of the individual letters: e.g., *cr* in *cr*ayon, and *pl* in *pl*ate.

Choral reading. Reading done orally by two or more pupils from the same passage at the same time.

Diagnosis. A careful investigation of a problem carried out by an individual to determine a proper sequence of remediation.

Digraph. These are two-letter combinations that represent a single sound which is unlike the sounds of the single letters composing the digraph: e.g., *sh* in *sh*elf, and *ch* in *ch*erry. In pronouncing a digraph sound the position of the mouth is not changed.

Diphthong. A combination of two vowel letters that are both heard in making a compound sound: e.g., *ow* in c*ow,* and *oy* in b*oy.* In pronouncing a diphthong sound the position of the mouth is changed.

Kinesthetic Method. The senses of touch, hearing, and seeing are used to teach reading. The approach usually involves tracing over words with the index and middle finger while sounding the part being traced.

Levels of Reading

> *Free reading level.* The child can function adequately without the teacher's help. Comprehension should average 90 percent and word recognition should average 99 percent.

---

* Edward W. Dolch, *Methods in Reading* (Champaign, Illinois: Garrard Publishing, 1955), pp. 373–74.

Instructional reading level. The child can function adequately with teacher guidance and yet be challenged to stimulate his reading growth. Comprehension should average 75 percent, and word recognition should average 95 percent.

Frustration reading level. The child cannot function adequately. The child often shows signs of tension and discomfort. Vocalization is often present. Comprehension averages 50 percent or less, and word recognition averages 90 percent or less.

Phonics. Letter sound relationships are applied to the teaching of reading, usually in a sequence similar to the following: learning of consonant sounds, initial, final, and middle, in that order; and then the learning of consonant blends, vowel sounds, vowel rules, and rules concerning the various sounds of *g, c,* and *x.*

Reading Programs

Developmental. The normal classroom instructional program followed by the teacher to meet the needs of pupils who are progressing at a normal rate in terms of their capacity.

Corrective. A program of instruction, usually conducted by a classroom teacher, within the class setting, to correct mild reading disabilities.

Remedial. A program of instruction used outside the regular classroom to teach specific developmental reading skills to underachievers.

Sight word. Any word that a reader has seen enough times in the past to enable him to recognize it instantly is a sight word. It should not be confused with *basic sight words.*

Structural analysis. Now often referred to as *morphology,* which is concerned with the study of meaning-bearing units such as word roots, prefixes, suffixes, possessives, plurals, word families, compound words, accent rules, and syllabication rules. Many authors disagree as to whether word families and syllabication rules come under the heading of *phonics* or *structural analysis.*

Word analysis skill. This skill involves the ability to derive the pronunciation and/or meaning of a word through phonics, structural analysis, or context clues.

Word recognition skill. A reader's ability to read a word which he has come into contact with previously. It may be through a process of associating it with its context, its configuration, or any other means that enables him to recognize a word.

Reading Diagnosis Sheet

NAME —————

GRADE —————

TEACHER —————

SCHOOL —————

#	1st Check	2nd Check	3rd Check	Description	Category
1				Word-by-word reading	ORAL READING
2				Incorrect phrasing	
3				Poor pronunciation	
4				Omissions	
5				Repetitions	
6				Inversions or reversals	
7				Insertions	
8				Substitutions	
9				Basic sight words not known	
10				Sight vocabulary not up to grade level	
11				Guesses at words	
12				Consonant sounds not known	
13				Vowel sounds not known	
14				Blends, digraphs or diphthongs not known	
15				Lacks desirable structural analysis	
16				Unable to use context clues	
17				Contractions not known	
18				Fails to comprehend	ORAL SILENT DIFFICULTIES
19				Unaided recall scanty	
20				Response poorly organized	
21				Low rate of speed	SILENT READING
22				High rate at expense of accuracy	
23				Voicing-lip movement	
24				Inability to skim	
25				Inability to adjust reading rate to difficulty of material	
26				Written recall limited by spelling ability	OTHER RELATED ABILITIES
27				Undeveloped dictionary skill	
28				Inability to locate information	

D—Difficulty recognized
P—Pupil progressing
N—No longer has difficulty

The items listed above represent the most common difficulties encountered by pupils in the reading program. Following each numbered item are spaces for notation of that specific difficulty. This may be done at intervals of several months. One might use a check to indicate difficulty recognized or the following letters to represent an even more accurate appraisal:

1. Word-by-Word Reading

RECOGNIZED BY

Pupil pauses after each word and does not allow the words to flow as they would in a conversation.

DISCUSSION

Word-by-word reading may be caused from an overdependence on phonics, failure to instantly recognize a number of sight words, or failure to comprehend. Young children who are beginning to read are often word-by-word readers. However, as a child's sight vocabulary continues to grow, he should lose this habit.

You should determine whether word-by-word reading is caused by habit, lack of word recognition, or lack of comprehension. This determination may be made as follows: Give the student something to read at a much lower reading level. If he continues to read poorly, his problem is caused by a bad habit. If the student immediately improves, it generally can be considered either a problem of comprehension or word recognition difficulty. You must then decide between these two problems. Ask the student questions over the more difficult material in which he was reading word-by-word. If he can answer approximately 75 percent of the questions correctly, then his problem probably lies in the area of word recognition. On the other hand, if he cannot answer approximately 75 percent of the questions correctly, he may be having trouble with comprehension. You may also wish to take a few of the sight words from the reading passage and put them on flash cards to see if he has instant recognition of these words in isolation. If the student has trouble with word recognition, the suggestions listed in items (A) through (D) will be helpful. If the difficulty lies in the development of poor reading habits, then the recommendations under items (E) through (L) will be more helpful. However, if the student is having difficulty with comprehension, then you should follow the suggestions listed under "Fails to Comprehend," Section 18, p. 88.

It should be remembered that a student can only read with fluency when he is thoroughly familiar with the vocabulary of the material he is required to read. Therefore, if a student is having difficulty with the vocabulary of material, you should not try the types of suggestions listed in items (E) through (L) which would treat the symptoms rather than the actual cause of the difficulty.

RECOMMENDATIONS

A.   Use reading material on a lower level of difficulty.

B.   Use materials with which the pupil is so familiar that the vocabulary presents no problem.

C.   Have the children write their own stories and read them aloud. Tape-record their reading of these stories and contrast it with their reading of more unfamiliar stories. Discuss the differences and their need for smooth, fluent reading.

D.   If word-by-word reading is caused by an insufficient sight vocabulary, you should follow the suggestions listed under "Incorrect Phrasing," Section 2, p. 9, Item (A), and those listed under "Sight Vocabulary Not Up to Grade Level," Section 10, p. 40.

E.   Have the pupil read in conjunction with a tape recording of the passage. It is often difficult for an adult to read with expression at a rate which will be comfortable for a child to follow. Some teachers prefer to use another good student at the same grade level to do the reading on the tape recorder.

F.   Provide experience in choral reading. This activity may be with as few as two pupils or as many as the entire class.

G.   Use mechanical devices which require the reader to attain a certain speed. If these mechanical devices are not available, the instructor may have the pupil pace his reading with his hand forcing his eyes to keep up with the pace set by the hand. (CAUTION! Do not allow the eye to pace the hand.) This may be done either orally or silently. Remember there is little emphasis on reading speed in the primary grades, and very little emphasis is given to teaching speed reading in the middle grades. Therefore, the mechanical devices are only to maintain a comfortable pace and not to increase speed per se.

H.   Give a series of timed silent reading exercises. The addition of the time factor will usually make the student aware of his habit. The same cautions pertaining to grade level should be observed here as for (G).

I.   Allow the pupil to choose stories which he feels are exciting and then let him read them aloud.

J.   Have the children read and dramatize conversation.

K.   Have the children read poetry. They should read it over until it becomes easy for them.

L.   Discuss reading as talk written down. Record several children's talk and then record the reading of dialogue. Let the children listen and compare the differences between talk and dialogue.

2. Incorrect Phrasing

RECOGNIZED BY

Pupil fails to pause or take a breath at the proper place in the material he is reading. The pupil often ignores punctuation, especially commas.

DISCUSSION

The causes of incorrect phrasing may be insufficient word recognition, insufficient comprehension, or the development of poor oral reading habits. You should first determine the cause. You could give the student an unorganized list of all the words from a passage he will read later. The passage should be at a reading level in which he is experiencing difficulty. If he does not know approximately 95 percent of the words in the list, it can be assumed that word recognition is contributing to the problem of incorrect phrasing. Or, you could have the student read the story from which the words came and then answer at least six questions from the story. If he continues to phrase incorrectly and fails to answer at least 75 percent of the questions, and yet knows 95 percent or more of the words, probably comprehension difficulties are a major contributor to the problem.

Reading material of a very low level given to the student is not too difficult for him if he has instant recognition of 95 percent or more of the words and can answer at least 75 percent of a series of questions over the passage. If the material is not too difficult for him in terms of vocabulary and comprehension, and he continues to phrase incorrectly, you may assume that the student has poor reading habits or does not understand the meaning of various punctuation marks. Remember that it is difficult for older students, even though they are good readers, to read stories on a primer or first grade level and then answer the type of comprehension questions commonly given to children who are actually working at this level. You should keep this in mind if it is necessary to use material of a very low level.

If insufficient word recognition skills are a contributing factor in incorrect phrasing, then the suggestions in items (A) through (F) should be beneficial. If incorrect phrasing is caused by poor oral reading habits or a failure to understand the meaning of certain punctuation marks, then the suggestions listed under (H) through (P) are appropriate. If, however, the cause of incorrect phrasing is a lack of word recognition or a lack of comprehension, consult (G) in the recommendations which will refer you to the appropriate section. If incorrect phrasing is caused by a lack of word recognition or a lack of comprehension, you would be treating only the symptom and not the cause by using the recommendations listed in (H) through (O).

RECOMMENDATIONS

A.   If it is determined that insufficient word recognition is a major contributor to the problem of incorrect phrasing, it is, of course, necessary to increase the student's sight vocabulary. A word becomes a sight word after it has been read many times. Some writers and researchers have estimated that it takes from twenty to seventy exposures to a word before it actually becomes a 'sight word'. A student who has not built up a sight vocabulary equivalent to his grade level must read and read and read in order to expose himself to as many new words as many times as possible. (See Appendix B for sources of high interest-low vocabulary books.)

B.   If is it determined that the cause of incorrect phrasing is a limited sight vocabulary, then the suggestions recommended under the section headed "Sight Vocabulary Not Up to Grade Level," Section 10, 40, will be helpful.

C.   Use the *Sight Phrase Cards* published by Garrard Press. (See Appendix B.)

D.   Compile lists of common prepositional phrases and have the students practice reading these phrases. (See Appendix F.)

E.   Listen to tape recordings of properly phrased reading while the student follows the same written material.

F.   Use material which presents no vocabulary problem, allowing the pupils to concentrate on phrasing without experiencing difficulty in word attack.

G.   If it is determined that the incorrect phrasing is caused by a lack of comprehension, then the recommendations under the section headed "Fails to Comprehend," Section 18, p. 88, will be helpful.

H.   Demonstrate proper phrasing by reading to the class.

I.   Review the meanings of various punctuation marks and discuss how these help the student to phrase properly. It often helps to draw an analogy between traffic signs and punctuation marks: i.e., commas are likened to yield the right-of-way signs and periods are likened to stop signs.

J.   Reproduce certain reading passages so that they are divided in phrases as in the following:

Fred and Mary   were on their way   to the movies.

In doing this, you may find that there is more carry-over if a space is left between the phrases rather than using a dash (—) or a slash (/) to separate the phrases.

K. Use mechanical devices (see Appendix B) which will force the reader to read more quickly. Be sure that whole phrases appear at the same time on the screen. You can easily make special filmstrips for this purpose. These can be used in a regular filmstrip projector, or they can be used in an automatic slide projector with one phrase of a story appearing on each slide. Remember the precaution stated previously in "Word-by-Word Reading" —mechanical devices used with young children should be set at a comfortable pace. They should not be used for reading speed per se.

L. Have the children read and dramatize conversation.

M. Provide choral reading with several readers who phrase properly.

N. Write sentences using crayons. Make each phrase a different color. After reading sentences in color have the students read them in black and white print. In the following example the different styles of type represent different colors.

Fred and Mary **were on their way**   to the movies.

O. Ditto or mimeograph songs. Have the students read these without the music.

P. Give students practice in oral reading phrases that each extend only to the end of the line. After practicing with oral phrases, phrases may be carried over into the next line; however, leave more than the normal amount of space between each phrase. Gradually go from this style to normal writing.

GAMES AND EXERCISES

Bouncing for Words

Purpose: To provide practice on basic sight words, other sight words, or sight phrases

Materials: Group-size (6″ x 3″) cards for the basic sight words, sight words in general, or sight phrases to be learned
A chair for each child
A basketball or volleyball

Procedure:

Each child is given one phrase card. He stands behind his chair and places his card face up on the seat of his chair. The leader, one of the children in the group, bounces the ball to the first child. As the child catches the ball, he says his phrase. If he says it correctly, he picks up his card. If he misses, the card remains on his chair. Play continues until all the children have a turn at their phrases. At the end of the game the children exchange cards and play again continues. Any child who could not say his phrase when he caught the ball is told the phrase, which he keeps until all words are exchanged at the end of the next game.

Use sight word cards instead of phrase cards, or use two teams. Instead of beginning with the children in a circle, have opposite teams face each other with eight or ten feet between each team. The leader then rotates the bounces between teams. The team with the least number of cards on their chairs after a certain number of sets or games is the winner.

Search

Purpose: To provide practice on the basic sight words or on phrasing

Materials: Three or more identical packs of word cards or three or more identical packs of sight phrase cards

Procedure:

Three or more children sit around a table, each with a pack of phrase or word cards which are identical to those of the rest of the players. One child looks at his pack and calls a phrase. The remaining players then see who can find the same phrase first. The child who does places the card faceup in the middle of the table and scores a point for himself. Play continues until a certain number of points are scored by an individual.

Pony Express

Purpose: To provide practice on phrasing

Materials: Pocket chart
Sight phrase cards

Procedure:

Fill a pocket chart with sight cards. Each word may represent a letter in the pony express saddlebag. The children come one at a time to claim their letters and read them to the rest of the class. After all cards have been removed from the chart the children exchange cards (letters) and begin again by mailing their letters (placing them back in the pocket chart).

A Phrasing Scope

Purpose: To provide practice in proper phrasing

Materials: Pieces of paper about 5″ wide
              A piece of cardboard a little larger than the strips of paper
              Two dowel pins about ½″ in diameter and 7″ long

Procedure:

Paste the pieces of paper into a long strip. Type a story, either original or from a book, on the strip. Type only one phrase on a line and double space the lines. Next, fold the piece of cardboard and seal the sides, leaving the top and bottom open. Cut a window near the top of the cardboard. Slide the strip of paper through the cardboard and attach a round stick (½″ dowel) at each end of the strip of paper. The pupil rolls the paper from the bottom to the top and reads the story as each phrase passes through the window's opening. See example following.

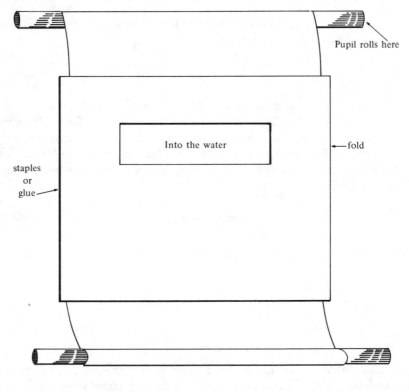

Sets

Purpose: To learn new phrases and to provide practice on reading those already known

Materials: Two sets of phrase cards, number used depending on the number of players; use four sets or four cards for each player

Procedure:

You deal out one set of phrase cards to players so that each player has four different phrases. You then place all duplicate phrases in a second set faceup in several rows on the table. Begin by pointing to a phrase and saying it. The student who has the matching phrase picks it up and says it as he places it in his hand to make a matching "set." Play continues until one player has a complete set. He must then read all the phrases in his hand as he lays down each set. If he cannot read them, play continues until another student has a complete matching set and can read them without help. The winner is, of course, the first student who obtains a complete matching set and is able to read all phrases from each set.

Drawing for Phrases

Purpose: To provide practice on reading basic sight words and phrases

Materials: Three small boxes
            1 inch squares of tagboard

Procedure:

In this game it is beneficial to have a disabled reader work with a good reader. Write a number of different prepositions on one inch squares of tagboard and place them in Box One. Use words such as *with, in, under,* and *over* that would fit with almost any noun. In Box Two place one inch tagboard squares with the words *the* and *a.* In Box Three place a few one inch tagboard squares with nouns on them such as *house,* and *chair.* Ask students to draw one square from each box to form a phrase. After all squares have been drawn and the phrases read, the squares may then be rearranged to form more phrases. You may wish to have the students write down the phrases to see who can get the most phrases. The written list is also useful for reviewing the phrases at a later date.

3. Poor Pronunciation

RECOGNIZED BY

Pupil fails to pronounce a word as it should be pronounced.

DISCUSSION

Mispronunciation of words is one of the more serious reading problems of retarded readers. The problem may be caused by several factors: (1) the pupil may be weak in his knowledge of phonics; (2) he may possess, but not use, a knowledge of phonics; (3) he may not understand diacritical markings; (4) he may be a careless reader; (5) he may have some speech defect or accent; and (6) he may have some hearing defect. In any case, a careful diagnosis is called for. The following paragraphs suggest ways of diagnosing the various reasons for poor pronunciation.

Child has weakness in phonics knowledge—Either the *CRS (Phonics Section)* * or the *El Paso Phonics Knowledge Survey* † can be used to quickly spot these areas of weakness in a student's knowledge of phonics. Teachers should be extra careful in selecting a phonics test to use. Extensive research at the Reading Center at the University of Texas at El Paso has shown that few, if any, group phonics tests examine what a student actually does in applying phonic word-attack skills. Therefore, such tests do not aid diagnostic teaching. This inadequacy is also true of some individual phonics tests. However, the *CRS* and *El Paso Survey* do require the student to respond to situations *similar to* actual application of skills.

Child has phonic knowledge but does not use—The two tests mentioned above actually test the ability to use phonics as well as phonics knowledge itself. The teacher may want to supplement test results by observing the ways in which the students attack or fail to attack new words.

Hearing defect—The *Auditory Discrimination Test* (see Appendix B) is easy to administer and will determine whether a student has difficulty discriminating be-

---

* Eldon E. Ekwall, "Phonics," *Corrective Reading System* (Glenview, Illinois: Psychotechnics, Inc., 1976).

† Eldon E. Ekwall, *A Teacher's Handbook in Diagnosis and Remediation in Reading* (Boston: Allyn and Bacon, Longwood Division, 1977), Chapter 5.

tween somewhat similar sounds. The inability to discriminate between certain sounds can lead to the mispronunciation of words. This knowledge, supplemented with informal hearing tests, such as determining whether the student hears a normal voice at the distance most children hear it, will help to decide whether a hearing defect is contributing to the reading difficulty. Pupils indicating difficulty in any of these areas should be further examined by a specialist.

No knowledge of diacritical markings—Informal exercises constructed by the teacher, based upon the dictionary may help. In an individual case this might simply include asking a student to read certain words from a dictionary in which the diacritical markings are shown. Once again, this type of task closely parallels that of reading.

Careless reading—You should stop the reader at a mispronounced word and ask him if he knows the correct pronunciation. If he usually does, the problem may be one of carelessness. This would still not exclude the possibility that training in various forms of word analysis might be beneficial.

Speech defect or accent—Ask the student to repeat sentences which are given orally. Use words which were mispronounced in previous reading. Words read incorrectly, but spoken correctly, are not speech problems.

Some students never seem to develop the ability to apply various rules which are required for the successful use of certain phonics skills. For this type of student the suggestions recommended under (B) may prove more satisfactory in helping word attack problems.

RECOMMENDATIONS

A. Teach the phonics skills in which a weakness is indicated by the phonics tests listed. (See Appendix B.) For sample exercises see "Games and Exercises," Section 12, p. 58.

B. Make lists of certain letter combinations which usually have the same sounds, such as *tion, ance,* and *edge.* Have the students keep their own lists.

C. Make lists of prefixes and suffixes; however, do not expect the children to learn the meaning of many of these. Focus only on the children being able to pronounce these affixes. (See list of suffixes and prefixes in Appendix G.)

D. Have the children make word cards or lists and build their own file of words which they habitually mispronounce. Allow for periodic, independent study of these words. An old shoe box makes an excellent file box for indexing word cards.

E. If the pupil possesses a knowledge of phonics that he doesn't use, give him exercises in which he is required to put the knowledge to use. For example:

1. Have him first pronounce *sent;* then give him a number of other words and nonsense words to pronounce which end in *ent,* such as d*ent,* p*ent,* and b*ent.* This exercise will give him practice in using various consonant sounds in conjunction with various word endings.

2. Do the same as (1), using consonant blends with various combinations; for example, pronounce *slash,* then give a number of other words and nonsense words ending in *ash,* such as cr*ash,* fl*ash,* and sc*ash.*

As the student reads, ask him to try to pronounce difficult words aloud. You should determine which sounds he knows but is not using. Use these sounds in constructing exercises similar to the two shown above or appropriate for improving the particular phase of phonics not being used.

F. Teach the child how to use the diacritical marks found in the dictionary. Try to find words and letter combinations similar to those missed by the child. For example, the child may use the short *o* sound in the word torn. To correct this you might construct an exercise such as the following.

Directions: Fill in the blanks with the correct word and then use your dictionary to mark the correct vowel sounds of the word you placed in the blank.

1. The old coat was *(wôrn).* (join   worn   to)

2. The old *(hôrn)* sounded as if it were new. (horn   man   sled)

3. They looked at the old man in *(scôrn).* (hurry   worry   scorn)

4. Please do not *(wôrry)* about the money. (open   worry   destroy)

G. When the pupil mispronounces a word in oral reading, call his attention to the correct pronunciation with as little fuss as possible. Ignoring the mistake tends to reinforce the wrong pronunciation with the pupil as well as with any other members of the class who are listening. Help the pupil to analyze the correct pronunciation.

H. Preceding the pupil's reading of difficult material, you can read it aloud or play a recording of it.

I. To teach certain sounds with which the pupil is having difficulty, do the following:

1. Set up pairs with only one different sound: e.g., *hit—heat.*

2. Make sure he can hear the sound differences.

3. Make sure he can say the word.

4. Use the word in a sentence and then have him say the single sound following that sentence.

J.   Have students hold their throats with their hands to feel the difference in vibration from one word to another or from one letter to another.

K.   Play games that deal with sounds. For example, the first student says, "I am a *ch*." The rest of the students then guess whether he is a chicken, chipmunk, etc. This gives all students many exposures to various word beginnings.

4.   Omissions

RECOGNIZED BY

Pupil omits certain words and/or phrases. Sometimes only letters are omitted.

DISCUSSION

Omissions in reading are usually caused by insufficient word recognition or word analysis skills and sometimes by the development of poor reading habits. Before beginning a program of help, you should try to determine the cause. You could have the pupil read material at the level in which he is making omissions and then note the percent of words omitted. Or, the pupil could be given a much easier passage. You should note whether omissions still occur. If omissions continue with approximately the same percent of occurrence, assume that they are a result of a bad habit. If, on the other hand, the percent of omissions markedly decreases, assume that word recognition and/or word analysis is a problem for the student.

Word analysis skills may be lacking in any of the following areas: phonics, structural analysis, use of context clues, and/or use of the dictionary (less often). If the problem stems from one of these difficulties, then the suggestions in items (A) through (E) will probably be of little or no value since the omissions are actually only symptoms of a larger problem in word analysis difficulties. It is then necessary to determine in which of the word analysis areas the pupil is deficient. The procedures and the suggestions recommended for each case are given in the following sections and pages:

> Phonics—Sections 12, p. 57; 13, p. 67; and 14, p. 73.
> Structural Analysis—Section 15, p. 75.
> Dictionary Skills—Section 26, p. 123.

If the student is able to analyze new words but does not have instant recognition of words which, for his grade level, should have become sight words, he lacks word recognition skills. It would then be necessary to help him build a sight vocabulary. To improve this area, as well as helping the child to recognize this problem, see "Sight Vocabulary Not Up to Grade Level," Section 10, p. 40.

If the child's problem is determined to be one of poor habits or carelessness, the suggestions listed under items (A) through (F) should be helpful.

RECOMMENDATIONS

A.   The reader's attention should be called to omissions when they occur. Making an immediate correction is the first step toward breaking the habit.

B.   Often a paper guide is helpful to younger readers. This guide may be a piece of paper approximately ½″ x 2″ with a tail on the bottom for a handle. (See the example.) Moving the guide along the line of print as the child reads will help him to keep his place. Remember the paper guide should be discarded as soon as possible.

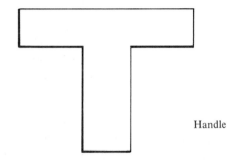

Handle

C.   If whole words or phrases are consistently skipped, the pupil may be required to point to each word as he reads it. *Make sure the reader reads the word he is pointing to and not several words ahead of or behind his finger.* You will discover a tendency for the reader to get ahead of or lag behind the word to which he is pointing. Having him pick up his finger slightly from word to word will help to improve this problem. This technique also should be stopped as soon as possible.

D.   Have several children choral read or let one child read with a tape recording of a reading passage.

E.   Ask detailed questions which require thorough reading. Ask about only a sentence or paragraph at a time. Students often will omit adjectives. In this case it is often helpful to give the student a list of questions such as, "Was the bear big or little?" "What color were the flowers?" The student will be forced to focus on adjectives that could otherwise easily be omitted.

F.   Giving help with word middles or endings often will help the problem of omitting these parts of words. The student's attention might be called to certain middles and endings, and you may make lists of common letter combinations.

G.   To focus atention to words omitted by the reader, tape-record a passage and then give the student a copy of the material as it is played back to him. Have him follow along pointing to each word as it is read. Have him circle all words omitted. After the reading, discuss possible reasons for his omitting the words and the importance of not doing so.

5. Repetitions

RECOGNIZED BY

Pupil re-reads words or phrases.

DISCUSSION

The cause of repetitions in students' reading is similar to the causes of omissions in reading—that is, poor word recognition skills, poor word analysis skills, and/or the development of a bad habit. A problem in word recognition skills is the more common of the causes. Pupils who are deficient in word recognition skills often make repetitions. It is common for them to repeat a word or phrase just preceding a word not instantly recognized by them. If the words not recognized by the pupil are ones which normally should be sight words for that pupil, it can be assumed that he is deficient in word recognition skills. In this case, the recommendations under "Sight Vocabulary Not Up to Grade Level," Section 10, p. 40, should be beneficial.

The problem of word analysis difficulties may be in any of the following areas: (1) phonics, (2) structural analysis, (3) use of context clues, and/or (4) use of the dictionary (less frequently). If the problem is in one of these areas, the recommendations suggested in items (A) through (E) would probably be of little or no value since the repetitions are only a symptom of the larger problems of word recognition or word analysis difficulties. You would need to determine in which area of word analysis the pupil was deficient. These procedures and the suggestions recommended in each case are given in the sections and pages as follows.

> Phonics—Sections 12, p. 57; 13, p. 67; and 14, p. 73.
> Structural Analysis—Section 15, p. 75.
> Context Clues—Section 16, p. 82.
> Dictionary Skills—Section 26, p. 123.

You can determine, to some extent, whether poor word recognition or word analysis skills is the cause of repetitions by having the pupil read material at the level in which he is making repetitions. Note the percent of words or phrases repeated. You might also give the pupil a much easier passage and note whether there is a definite decrease in the percent of repetitions. If there is, the problem is probably insufficient word recognition or word analysis skills. If, on the other hand, a student continues making as many repetitions as he did on the more difficult passage, then the problem is probably a bad habit.

If you determine that the problem results from bad habits, then the recommendations listed under items (A) through (F) should prove beneficial. Also, following the suggestions listed under (F) and (H) may give the pupil the confidence he needs to help break the habit.

RECOMMENDATIONS

A.   Call the repetitions to the student's attention. This is the initial step in breaking the bad habit.

B.   Have the student read with a tape recording of the material in the reading passage.

C.   Have the students choral read.

D.   Use mechanical devices which are designed to project a certain number of words per minute and which prevent the reader from regressing. (See Appendix B.) When working with children in the primary grades, you should not worry about speed itself. You must make sure the instrument does not move at a rate too fast for the normal reading rate of the reader.

E.   Have the student set a certain pace with his hand and keep up with this pace as he reads. Do not let the eyes pace the hand.

F.   To focus attention to words repeated by the reader, tape-record a passage read and then give the student a copy of the material as it is played back to him. Have him follow along pointing to each word. Have him underline any words as they are repeated. After completing the passage discuss any reasons that he believes are causing him to repeat words or phrases.

G.   Provide easier or more familiar material in which the vocabulary presents no problem.

H.   Let the students read the material silently before attempting to read orally.

6. *Inversions or Reversals*

RECOGNIZED BY

Pupil reads words from right to left instead of the normal left to right sequence, e.g., *was* for *saw,* or *pot* for *top.*

Pupil reads letters in reverse, e.g., *d* for *b,* or *p* for *g.*

Pupil makes partial reversals in words (the letters within words), e.g., *ant* for *nat.*

Pupil reverses words with in sentences, e.g., the *rat* chased the *cat,* instead of, the *cat* chased the *rat.*

DISCUSSION

Reversals may be caused by a number of factors. The child may have failed to develop a left to right eye movement, or a left to right reading pattern. He may suffer from mixed dominance, or he may fail to realize that the order or position in which letters appear does make a difference. Other possible factors are immaturity, improper instruction, and rapid reading.

Observation and questioning will, in some cases, help locate the cause of the reversals. However, unless the problem is a very difficult one caused by a neurological dysfunction, you need not be concerned with which of the above causes is the major contributor. The recommendations given would tend to be the same in any case. If, on the other hand, the pupil fails to respond to the recommendations, you may want to do a much more thorough diagnosis. Since the diagnosis, as well as the treatment, can be somewhat difficult, it is best to refer the pupil to a psychologist or neurologist if the pupil has not improved after several weeks of instruction.

RECOMMENDATIONS

A.   Emphasize left-to-right in all reading activities. The following methods may be helpful:

   1.   Cover words or sentences with hand or a card. Read the word or sentence as it is uncovered. The student may also find it helpful to

make a window marker as shown following. The child uses it as he would a regular marker, but lets the line of print show through the slot.

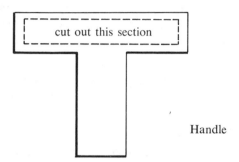

2. Underline the word or sentence, sounding the word as it is underlined or reading the sentence as it is underlined.

3. Teach the child to pace his reading with his hand, practicing a left to right movement.

4. Draw arrows pointing from left to right under troublesome words.

B. Have the pupils make word cards (about 8½″ x 3″). Let the students trace these troublesome words with the index and middle fingers (both at once) while they sound the parts of the word. Then have them write the word from memory. Keep files on these cards (an old shoe box will do as a file box).

C. Use flash cards to give practice on troublesome words. A system such as mentioned in (B) is suitable, with flash cards used in addition to the student's own study.

D. Let the child use a typewriter to practice words with which he has difficulty. This will enable him to see the word formed from left to right.

E. Pair the letters which are causing difficulty (such as *p* and *q*). Have the pupil trace the letters with his index and middle fingers, sounding each letter as it is traced.

F. If whole words are reversed, you can have the pupil trace the word and then attempt to write it from memory.

G. If the pupil reads very rapidly, have him read more slowly. Determine if the percentage of reversals decreases. If it does, have the pupil practice somewhat slower reading. Do this only if it is very evident that rapid reading is contributing to the reversal problem.

H. Use a magnetic board with three-dimensional letters. Have the pupil manipulate letters to form words commonly reversed.

I.   Write in pairs the words sometimes reversed (was–*saw*, net–*ten*, war–*raw*, trap–*part*). Use one word in a sentence and ask pupils to point to or write the word used.

J.   Use a colored letter at the beginning of words commonly confused. Discontinue this practice as soon as the word no longer presents any difficulty for the child.

K.   Blindfold the pupil and form letters or words with which he is having difficulty using three-dimensional letters. Have the pupil trace the letter and say it as you trace it on his back, making sure that your finger follows the same part of the letter on his back that his does in tracing the three-dimensional letter.

L.   To help make the student aware of the importance of sequence of words commonly reversed, place one word commonly reversed over another. Then have the pupil draw lines from the first letter of the top word to the first letter of the bottom word. Have him say each letter as he begins drawing the line from it and each letter as the line reaches it. See example following.

$$
\begin{array}{cc}
\text{o \quad n} & \text{s \quad a \quad w} \\
\big| \quad \big| & \big| \quad \big| \quad \big| \\
\text{n \quad o} & \text{w \quad a \quad s}
\end{array}
$$

M.   Write two words commonly reversed side by side. Ask the student to number the letters in the first word by placing a number under each letter. Then ask him to assign the same numbers to the letters in the second word. See example following.

$$
\begin{array}{cccc}
\text{s \ a \ w} & \text{w \ a \ s} & \text{o \ n} & \text{n \ o} \\
1 \ 2 \ 3 & 3 \ 2 \ 1 & 1 \ 2 & 2 \ 1
\end{array}
$$

7. Insertions

RECOGNIZED BY

Pupil adds words which are not present in the sentences. For example, in the sentence, "The dog chased the little boy," the pupil may add *big* to make the sentence read, "The *big* dog chased the little boy."

DISCUSSION

One of the most common causes of a pupil's inserting words in sentences seems to be the pupil's lack of comprehension. It is also possible that the pupil's oral language development surpasses his reading level, or he may be careless. Insertions that make sense within the context of the sentence indicate the student's awareness of the material he is reading. In this case, you may assume the insertions are caused from either carelessness or oral language development beyond the reading level. When the insertions do not make sense within the context of the sentence, you may assume that comprehension problems are involved. The recommendations listed in (A) through (F) are appropriate when the problem is carelessness or the oral language development surpasses reading ability. If the cause is sufficient comprehension, then the recommendations suggested in "Fails to Comprehend," Section 18, p. 88, are recommended.

RECOMMENDATIONS

A. Call the pupil's attention to each insertion. Sometimes he is not aware of the habit. Allowing him to continue only provides reinforcement for his mistakes.

B. Ask questions which require an exact answer. If the student usually follows a certain pattern in making insertions (such as adding adjectives) you may wish to provide questions for him to look at before he reads the story. Focus the questions on a correct reading of the material as it is written. Use questions such as, "Does it say how big the frog was?" "Was it a sunny warm day, a sunny cold day, or just a sunny day?"

C. Have the pupils choral read.

D. Have the pupil read along with a passage that has been tape recorded.

E.   If the pupil makes many insertions, have him point to each word as he reads. Have him lift his finger up and bring it down on each word as it is read. Do not allow him to continue the technique after the habit has disappeared.

F.   Play a tape recording in which the student made insertions. Ask the student to follow the written passage. Have him write on the written passage the insertions that were made on the oral reading of that material. Use the student-corrected passages as a basis for discussing the problem.

8. Substitutions

RECOGNIZED BY

Pupil substitutes one word for another.

DISCUSSION

The child who substitutes one word for another is probably either a careless reader or a reader who has not developed adequate word recognition skills. The substitutions made by many readers are nearly correct within the context of the material being read: e.g., "The man drove the *automobile*" might be read "The man drove the *car*." If these minor mistakes do not appear too often, it may be best to ignore the problem. If, however, they consistently occur, some steps should be taken. Substitutions which are not in the proper context of the sentence usually are caused by word recognition difficulty. When help is given with word recognition skills, the problem of substitutions usually disappears. You should determine whether substitutions are caused by carelessness or insufficient word recognition skills and plan help accordingly. You should note whether certain substitutions appear only in the child's reading or whether they occur in his speech as well.

If the substitutions made by the pupil are not in the proper context of the sentence, they are probably caused by the lack of word recognition skills. In that case, the recommendations under items (A) through (E) should be helpful. If, however, substitutions are caused by carelessness, the recommendations under items (E) through (K) should be helpful.

RECOMMENDATIONS

A. Make flash cards of words which cause difficulty. Ask the pupil to keep a file of these words.

B. Work on the beginning syllables and/or sounds that cause difficulty. (See Appendix A.)

C. Use the difficult words in multiple choice sentences, such as the examples following:

    1. John's father gave him a (watch, witch, water) for his birthday.

2. He (though, thought, through) he would be the tallest boy in the class.

3. He asked his father (what, where, when) they would leave.

4. She said, "The books belong to (them, that, this)."

D. Use the words in sentences where the student must complete the word in order to make the sentence sensible. For example:

1. Can you tell me wh_____ they will be home?

2. Does th_____ book belong to Dwight?

3. The stunt driver drove his car t_____ the wall of fire.

4. Cindy said, "That funny l_____ dog belongs to me."

E. Sometimes students feel they must make a continual response while they are reading. When such students do not know a strange word, they are likely to substitute whatever word comes into their heads rather than take the time to use analysis skills. Assure these students that they will be given ample amount of time to attack a word before you or a classmate tells them the word.

F. Call attention to the mistake and correct it when it occurs.

G. Have the pupils choral read.

H. Have the pupils read along with a passage that has been tape recorded.

I. Ask questions about the subject mater which will reflect the pupil's mistakes. Have him read to make corrections.

J. Have the pupils follow a printed copy of what they have read as it is played on a tape recorder. As they listen, have them circle words for which substitutions were made. Use this student-corrected material when discussing the problem.

K. Some students, especially when they are under pressure during a test or in a situation somewhat different from their normal environment, will feel pressure to read rather rapidly. If you sense that a student is reading more rapidly than he should or normally does, then stop him and explain that it is not necessary for him to read faster than usual.

9.   Basic Sight Words Not Known

RECOGNIZED BY

Pupil is unable to read some or all of the basic sight words—those words of high utility that make up from 50 to 65 percent of the words in most reading material. The percent would, of course, be higher when written at a lower reading level.

DISCUSSION

There are several lists of the common or basic sight words. One is provided in Appendix H. These are the words which make up half or more of the reading matter in elementary reading material. Since these words appear frequently, it is important that a child recognize them instantly. If children do not have these words in their sight vocabulary, or cannot recognize them instantly, they cannot become fluent readers. Children often confuse certain basic sight words, especially those with similar beginnings: e.g., *wh*en, *wh*ere, and *wh*at, or *th*is, *th*at, and *th*ose.

The test of the basic sight words often is given by showing the pupil four words and asking him to circle or underline the words you pronounce. The ability to distinguish a word from a choice of four words is not, however, the same as the ability to pronounce the word in print. You frequently will find that older students can score 100 percent on a basic sight word test if given in this manner, but that the same students may not be able to pronounce many of the same words when they are asked to read them.

A better way to determine which words are not known by a pupil is to point at the words and have him say them. Circle or underline the words not known on a separate list that you keep. A still better method is to have each of the basic sight words on a separate card. Ask the pupil to pronounce the words as you show each word card. Each card should be exposed to the student for a period of about one second. The unknown words are put into one pile and those known into another. You or the student may compile a list of those not known.

You will be able to find out when particular sight words should be known by a student by checking Appendix H. The first digit of the designation refers to grade level, and the second digit after the decimal refers to the month. These digits designate the point at which these words should have been mastered by the student.

RECOMMENDATIONS

A.   Have the pupil write troublesome words on cards (8½″ x 3″). Trace the word using the index and middle finger. Sound parts of words as it is traced. After the pupil knows the word, it should no longer be sounded. (Some words do not sound as they are spelled. In this case the sounding part should be omitted.) Use cards to form sentences. Also give sentences with the sight words omitted. Have the pupil fill in blanks with the appropriate word from his pile of cards.

B.   Use the sight words causing difficulty in sentences. Underline the words causing difficulty as in the following examples:

     1.   I thought it was you.

     2.   I could not go even though I have time.

     3.   He ran right through the stop sign.

C.   Pictures can be used to illustrate some words such as: *play, wash, work, small,* and *sing.* Use a picture with a sentence describing it and the sight word underlined, or have the children make picture dictionaries. See examples which follows.

The thimble is small.

The dog likes to play.

D.   Have the pupil write troublesome words on a card (8½″ x 3″) and then pantomime the action described by the word: e.g., *pull, sleep, ride, jump.*

E.   Place one word in a line which is different from the rest. Ask the pupil to circle the one that says "what": e.g., *when, when, what, when, when.*

F.   Use words commonly confused in multiple choice situations. Have the pupils underline the correct word. See examples which follow.

     1.   He wanted to (walk, wash) his clothes.

     2.   He didn't know (when, what) to do.

     3.   He put it over (there, their).

     4.   I (well, will) go with you.

G. Have the pupil read the entire sentence, look at the beginning and end of the word, and then try to pronounce it on the basis of its context and configuration.

H. For slow learners who have a great deal of difficulty with certain words, try cutting letters from sandpaper or velvet so that the child can "feel" the word as he pronounces it. Follow the same procedure described in (A). For certain students it is helpful to put a thin layer of salt or fine sand in a shoe box lid and let them practice writing the word in the salt or sand.

I. Place a piece of paper over a piece of screen wire such as the wire used on screen doors of a house. Before doing this it is a good idea to cover the edges of the screen wire with book binding tape so that the rough edges do not cut anyone. Writing on the paper on the screen wire with a crayon will leave a series of raised dots. Have the student trace basic sight words in this manner and then have him trace over the words, saying them as they are traced.

J. Each day pass out a few basic sight words on cards to students. Each student in turn goes to the board and writes his word. The class should try to say it aloud. After it is pronounced correctly, have them write it in a notebook. On some days have students select words from their notebooks and write them on the chalkboard. Then ask various members of the class to say these words.

GAMES AND EXERCISES

(Also see "Games and Exercises" for improving sight vocabulary, Section 10, p. 41. Many of the games and exercises listed there are appropriate for improving knowledge of basic sight words.)

Dominoes

Purpose: To provide practice in word discrimination

Materials: Flash cards, divided in half by a line, in which a different word is on each side of the card. (See examples.) Make sure that the words are repeated several times on different cards.

the	what

and	the

a	and

go	a

Procedure:

After mixing the cards, the game proceeds the same as dominoes. The child pronounces the word as he matches it.

Word Order

Purpose: To provide practice on basic sight words and/or other sight words, or to provide practice in recognition of phonic elements

Materials: Dittoed sheets of words arranged in the same manner as the following example.

A. why _____   B. c _____
    what _____   d _____
    when _____   g _____
    where _____   b _____
    which _____   f _____

C. cat _____   D. sound _____
    mule _____   frog _____
    cage _____   wolf _____
    pill _____   rabbit _____
    duck _____   pass _____

Procedure:

Tape-record or read words or sounds to the children who have the dittoed sheets. Each set should, however, concentrate on practice in only one area. The directions for the preceding sets would be similar to the following example.

Set A: Number the words in the order which they are read.

Set B: Number the letters that correspond with the same beginning sound that you hear in the following words (in the order they are given): *book, food, good, can, dog.*

Set C: Put number *1* in front of the word with a long *a.*
          Put *2* in front of the word with a short *u.*
          Put *3* in front of the word with a short *a.*
          Put *4* in front of the word with a long *u.*
          Put *5* in front of the word with a short *i.*

Set D: Number the words, in the order they are given, that have ending letter sounds. Give the following sounds: *f, t, g, d, s.*

Passport

Purpose: To provide practice on the basic sight words and/or other sight words

Materials: Use either group-size (6" x 3") or individual-size cards (3" x 1½").
One set is given to the group of children and one is kept by the captain, who is usually a child who knows the words quite well.

Procedure:

Each child is given one or several words (passports). In order to get aboard the
boat, they must show their passports to the captain. When the captain calls their port
(their word or words) from his deck of cards, the person who has a card matching
the captain's must show it to him to get off the boat.

Variation in Procedure:

The same game can be played with the sound of the consonants and vowels. In
this case, the captain has word cards and the child who has a letter matching the
sound of the first letter in the word called by the captain shows his passport (letter)
and is allowed to leave the boat.

Word in the Box

Purpose: To provide review and reinforcement on words that present problems
to pupils

Materials: A large box
Word cards with words on them that have given the children trouble
in their reading

Procedure:

The children sit in a circle around the box. You either read or play a tape recording of a story. Before hearing the story, each child is given a card on which there
is a word from the story. When that word is read in the story the child says
"_____ goes in the box" and throws the word in the box. The child then is given
another word so that he may continue in the game.

Word Football

Purpose: To provide practice on the recognition of basic sight words and/or
other sight words

Materials: A large sheet of drawing paper
A small replica of a football
Word cards

Procedure:

Draw a football field on a large piece of paper. The game begins at the fifty-yard
line where the football is placed. The word cards are then placed faceup on the

table, and two children, or two teams, take turns reading them. If a child reads a word correctly, he moves the ball ten yards toward the opponent's goal. If he reads the word incorrectly, it is considered a fumble and the ball goes ten yards toward his own goal. Each time the ball crosses into the end zone, six points are scored. The scoring side then gets to read one more word to try for the extra point.

Word Checkers

Purpose: To provide practice in word recognition or phonic sounds

Materials: Checkerboard
Small squares of paper with sight words or phonic sounds on them

Procedure:

You or the child covers the black squares with the words. The game is played the same as regular checkers, but the player must say the word which appears on the square before a checker is placed on that space.

Variation in Procedure:

Phonic sounds may be used instead of words.

Pack of Trouble

Purpose: To discover which children do not know certain words and to provide special help in such cases

Materials: Word cards using the vocabulary currently being studied
Blank cards on which you can print words

Procedure:

You flash word cards to individual students and ask them to pronounce the words as quickly as possible. Whenever a child misses a word, he is given that word and makes a copy of it to keep. He then can give the original back to you. Each child develops his own pack of trouble which he can use for study with another individual or with a small group. As soon as he masters a word he may give it back to you. The idea is, of course, to keep your pack of trouble as small as possible.

Climbing the Word Ladder

Purpose: To provide practice on basic sight words, sight words in general, or on sight phrases

Materials: A number of card packs of ten words. On the cards can be basic sight words, other sight words, or sight phrases.
A small ladder that will hold ten cards. The rungs of the ladder may be made from wood ¾″ round and the vertical poles from wood of 1″ x 2″. See illustration following.

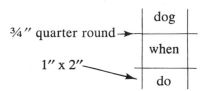

Procedure:

Each child receives a pack of cards and tries to try to climb the ladder with them. Cards are laid on each rung of the ladder. The child then tries to climb it by saying the words. After the child has mastered his own words, let him exchange packs and begin again with new words.

Hands Up (Words)

Purpose: To provide practice on recognition of basic sight words, and/or other sight words

Materials: Group-size cards (6″ x 3″)

Procedure:

Quickly flash a word card around the group allowing each child to see it. The child whose turn it is to pronounce the word then has a chance to do so. If he pronounces the word correctly, he is given the word card. If he does not, he is required to raise his hand. When the next card is flashed the second child has a chance to say it. If, however, the child who has his hand up can pronounce the word before the second child, he gets the card and may put his hand down. The second child then receives a chance at another word. If, of course, he misses that word, he must hold up his hand, and so on. The object is to get the most cards. There may also be a number of children with their hands up at any one time. If this is the case, the one who pronounces the word first gets the card.

Surprise Words

Purpose: To reinforce knowledge of the basic sight words and/or sight words

Materials: Word cards to fit pocket chart
              A pocket chart

Procedure:

Fill the pocket chart with words which are being studied currently. Turn the cards so that only the backs are showing. The children take turns coming up to the chart and taking a surprise word. If they can pronounce the word, they get to keep it; if they cannot, they must leave it in the chart. The child with the most words at the end of a certain time period wins the game.

Gamble for Words

Purpose: To provide practice on either basic sight words and/or other sight words

Materials: Pocket chart
              Cards with either the basic sight words or any sight word on them
              A die

Procedure:

Place the words to be worked on in a pocket chart or on the shelves of a pegboard unit. One child then rolls a die. He may pick up the same number of cards from the chart as the number indicated on the die. He must, however, be able to say each word as he picks it up. The turn then passes to another child. The object is, of course, to see who can get the most words. This game may be played using either a student vs. student approach or a team vs. team approach. You may set a time limit for the game or limit the game to a certain number of refills of the pocket chart.

Word Match

Purpose: To provide practice on word recognition

Materials: A pack of word cards in which every card has a word on it that is duplicated; that is, there should be two cards for each word to be used. The number of cards will depend on the number of players involved.

Procedure:

The players are each dealt four cards which are placed faceup in front of each player. Five cards are then placed faceup in the middle of the table. The remainder of the pack in placed facedown in the middle of the table. If the first player has a card that matches any of the five face-up cards in the middle of the table, he picks it up, pronounces the word, and keeps the pair, placing them facedown in front of him. He may continue playing until he can make no more pairs. He then draws to fill his hand to four cards and replaces the five face-up cards on the table. If, in this process, cards which match are drawn and placed on the table, they are left for the individual who has the next turn. Play continues to the first player on the left. If a player can match a card in the middle of the table, but cannot pronounce the word, he must place his card on the card in the middle and leave it. If the following player can pronounce the word, he receives the pair. The winner is the person with the most cards when all the cards are paired.

Rolling for Words

Purpose: To teach and provide practice on basic sight words

Materials: Three colors of construction paper
A die
Three small boxes

Procedure:

Cut the colored construction paper into one inch squares. Print a basic sight word on each square. Put the squares into separate boxes according to the color of the paper. You may wish to put primer words on one color, first grade words on another color, etc. The players throw the die to see who starts the game. The student with the higher number starts by selecting as many words from any one box as the number on the die. If he fails to say any one of the words he loses all the words from that turn and, after being told the missing word by the teacher, returns the words to the appropriate box. Play continues to the first player's left. The winner is the one with the most words when all three boxes are empty at the end of the game.

Finding Rhyming Words

Purpose: To teach and reinforce basic sight words

Materials: Flash cards from basic sight words from which rhyming words can be made
A pocket chart

Procedure:

Place the flash cards in the pocket chart. You then say, "I want a word that rhymes with *fat*." Students take turns looking for a word to rhyme with the one given by you. If the student cannot find the word, he is given a word to hold by you or by another student who knows it. The winners are those students who are holding no words at the end of the game.

Finding Phrases

Purpose: To reinforce knowledge of the basic sight words

Materials: Pocket chart
            Basic sight word cards 3″ x 8½″

Procedure:

Place the words in the pocket chart to make four or five phrases (for example, *is in* and *wants to go*). Then say a sentence such as, "The boy wants to go." Students take turns going to the pocket chart and placing their hands on the phrase from the sentence and reading it. If a student fails to read it correctly, he must take the cards from that phrase to be studied. The object is to have no cards at the end of the game.

The Password

Purpose: To provide practice on especially difficult basic sight words

Materials: Straight or safety pins
            3″ x 8½″ cards

Procedure:

Take a group of students who are having trouble with the same basic sight words. Write one of the basic sight words on each card and go over the words thoroughly with the children. Then pin one card on each student. Throughout the day, whenever one student must deal with another or whenever you wish to get a response from that student, call the basic sight word written on the student's card rather than his name before that student is to respond. This can be done daily with different groups of words and students.

Concentration

Purpose: To develop the ability to recognize basic sight words

Materials: Basic sight word flash cards in which each card has a duplicate

Procedure:

Find ten to twelve cards and their duplicate cards (total of twenty to twenty-four). Shuffle the cards and lay them facedown on the table. The first student turns up a card and says the word. He then turns up another card trying to find the duplicate of the first one turned up. If the second card is not a duplicate of the first, or if the student does not know the word, he turns them facedown and the next student takes his turn. If a student is able to turn up one card, say the word, and then turn up the duplicate of that card, he gets to keep the pair. As play continues, students will, of course, find it easier to find matching pairs. The person with the most pairs at the end of the game wins.

10. Sight Vocabulary Not Up to Grade Level

RECOGNIZED BY

Pupil fails to instantly recognize words thought to be common for or below his own grade level. (Failure not limited to words commonly called *basic* sight words.)

DISCUSSION

In advancing from grade to grade, the pupil should increase his sight vocabulary at each grade level. A pupil's sight vocabulary is not up to grade level unless he can correctly pronounce 95 percent of the words in a book or textbook at his grade level. The pupil who, for some reason, has not developed an adequate number of sight words at each grade level is greatly handicapped since he must analyze many more words than a normal reader. This child is more likely to encounter reading material on his frustration level.

You should not determine whether a library book is at a certain grade level from the publisher's recommendation unless that recommendation has been made on the basis of one of the better reading formulas. You can, however, expect a textbook to be written at approximately the level for which it was intended. Even when using a textbook at a certain level to determine whether a student is retarded in his sight vocabulary you should take passages from several parts of the book to insure an accurate diagnosis.

RECOMMENDATIONS

A. Have the pupil read as widely as possible on his free or low instructional level. In doing so he will learn new words from their context. (See Appendix B for high interest-low vocabulary books.)

B. Have the pupil start a card file of new words. Write the word and the definition on the front of the card. On the back, write the word in its proper context in a sentence (never write just the word and the dictionary definition alone).

C. Many basal readers have lists of new words introduced in the book. Sometimes these are at the end of each chapter. Determine the grade level appropriate to begin with (where the child knows approximately 95 percent of the words in these lists) and read stories from basal readers to him. Discuss the meanings of new words as you come to them. Following this, have the child read the stories. Give him help when it is needed.

D.   Build on the pupil's background of experience as much as possible. Use films, filmstrips, records, tape recordings, or anything which will build his listening-speaking vocabulary. This will make it easier for him to acquire new words through context clues.

E.   Use picture word cards on which the unknown word appears under a picture illustrating that word. When making these it is also helpful to use the word in a sentence as well as by itself. Have the pupils work in pairs or small groups to learn these new words from the word cards. Have the children work cooperatively to build a file of pictures representing scenes, action events, and so forth in stories. Before the children begin to read the new stories, discuss these picture files with them. Pictures may also be put in scrapbooks and pages may be divided into sections (represented by letters) on numbered pages. You can then make a tape recording to go along with the scrapbook. The script for the tape recording might read as follows:

> On page three of the scrapbook in Picture A you see a picture of a waterfall. In the story you are going to read today, a man goes over a waterfall in a boat. The boat probably looks about like the one in Picture B. The men have been camping in the woods and probably look like the men in Picture C.

Put the children at listening stations and have them prepare for reading a story by listening to these tapes and looking at the scrapbooks.

F.   Have the pupils pantomime certain words such as *write, hear,* and *walk.* Make sure the pupils see the word immediately before, during, and/or after seeing it pantomimed.

G.   Teach the pupils one method that they can follow consistently in attacking a new word. For example:

1.   Look at the word.
2.   See if any part of it looks like a word you already know.
3.   How does it begin? How does it end?
4.   Read the other words in the line and see what you think it should be.
5.   Listen for the word in the rest of the lesson or when others speak.

GAMES AND EXERCISES

Sight Words in Context

Purpose: To provide practice on sight words and/or use of context clues

Materials: Pocket chart
Group-size word cards
Tape recorder

Procedure:

Place eight to ten words in the bottom pockets of the pocket chart. These should be new words on which you wish to provide practice. Play a tape recording of a short story which uses the words in the bottom rows of the pocket chart. Say the word and at the same time ring a bell or sound a buzzer. At the signal, the student picks the correct card from the eight to ten choices in the bottom rows and places it in the top row of the pocket chart. Be sure to pause briefly after the word to give the student a chance to look for it. You will need to allow for longer pauses at the beginning of the story when there are more words at the bottom of the pocket chart. The cards should be placed in order from left to right beginning with Row One. When the top row is full, they then begin the left-to-right sequence in Row Two and so on until all cards have been transferred from the bottom to the top of the chart. After all the words are transferred from the bottom to the top of the chart, you can check the words with the student in the following manner: "In Row One, the first word is _____, the next word is _____," etc. This makes the exercise self-correctional when it is programmed on the tape along with the rest of the exercise.

Variation in Procedure:

Instead of saying the word as a bell or buzzer rings, merely ring the buzzer and let the student find the word from context.

Zingo

Purpose: To provide practice in the recognition of the basic sight words or other sight words

Materials: A number of word cards (7″ x 7″) with twenty-five squares, each of which has a different sight word on it
A list of each of the sight words
A number of kernels of corn, buttons, or beans

Procedure:

This game is played like bingo. Read a word from the word list and ask the children to hunt for that word on their word (Zingo) cards. When they find the word pronounced by you, then place a kernel of corn or some other marker on it. The first child to get five spaces filled in any direction is the winner. After a child has won he should pronounce the words covered by the marker to you. This will insure that the children not only recognize words by sight, but that they also can say them themselves.

Construct your word list so that you can allow various individuals to win if you so desire: e.g., Zingo Card 3 may win by saying words 2, 8, 10, 12, and 15. Although this is a pre-arranged game, it will enable you to allow the pupils who need motivation to win.

Racetrack

Purpose: To provide practice in recognition of basic sight words and/or other sight words

Materials: A large sheet of drawing paper
Two duplicate sets of individual-size word cards (3″ x 1½″)
Two toy automobiles

Procedure:

Draw an oval track on the drawing paper to resemble a racetrack. Be sure to put in a start and finish line. Divide the track into sections in which there are printed drill words. Each of the two players has a toy automobile which is placed on the starting line of the track. Each player has a set of small word cards which are a duplicate of those of the opposing player and also duplicate the words on the racetrack. Each player places his pile of cards faceup. One player then reads the word on his top card. If the word is the same as the one in the first space of the racetrack his auto is moved up. If it is not, he may not move. His card is placed on the bottom of the deck and the other player takes his turn. The winner is the first player to go around the racetrack to the finish line. Be sure cards are shuffled well before each game.

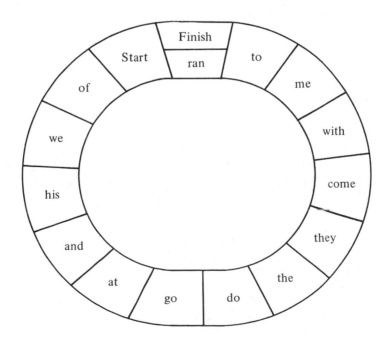

Treasure Hunt

Purpose: To provide practice on the basic sight words and/or other sight words

Materials: Sight word cards with a word on one side and phrases on the backs
which say: "Go to a word that starts with *c*," or "Go to a word that
starts with *w*."

Procedure:

A number of word cards are placed on the top of the children's desks with sight
words showing. Two or three people are given different cards that say: "Go to a
word that starts with *w*," etc. The children immediately start to hunt for words with
the beginning letters as indicated. When they find them they must say the word that
starts with the letter they were hunting for. They may then turn it over and get
directions for the next step in the treasure hunt. The last card should have a picture
of a treasure chest on the back of it instead of directions to look further. You will,
of course, need to arrange your card sets so that each child goes through the same
number of steps.

Donkey

Purpose: To provide practice on basic sight words and/or other sight words

Materials: Make a deck of cards using one new word causing difficulty on each.
You may use any number of players. In the deck you should include
three to five cards with the word *donkey* written on them.

Procedure:

Deal all cards to the players facedown. The players then take turns turning up a
card, pronouncing it, and placing it in a pool in the middle of the table. When the
"donkey" card appears the player drawing it says *donkey* and throws it in the center
of the table. All the players try to grab the "donkey" card. The one who gets it
may keep it and all cards that have been thrown into the pool. The winner of the
game is the player who ends up with all of the cards or the most cards when all
"donkey" cards have been drawn.

The Head Chair

Purpose: To provide practice on the recognition of the basic sight words and/or
other sight words

Materials: Group-size word cards (6" x 3")

Procedure:

Mark one chair in the circle and call it the *head chair*. Play begins when you flash a card to the person in the head chair. A child can stay in his chair only until he misses a word. When he misses a word he goes to the end chair and all the children from this child to the end chair move up one chair. Continue around the circle from the head chair to the end chair. The object is to try to end up in the head chair.

Variation in Procedure:

If you are working with a relatively small group, have all of the chairs facing you. This will enable all of the children to see all of the words.

Cops and Robbers

Purpose: To provide practice on the recognition of basic sight words and/or other sight words

Materials: Tagboard
             Word cards

Procedure:

On a piece of tagboard construct an irregular course of dots and then connect the dots with lines. At points along the course place hideouts, dried up waterholes, deserts, etc. The game is played with two children—one a bank robber, one a police officer. The bank robber will place his marker on the course as far from the officer's marker as possible. The game begins with each player turning over a word card from a pack placed facedown on the table. He reads the word on the card and then moves the number of dots denoted by a number appearing in one of the corners of the word card. The robber tries to avoid the officer. The game ends when the robber is captured. A more difficult game can be made by increasing the number of moves allowed according to the difficulty of the word given.

Team Sight Word Race

Purpose: To provide drill on basic sight words and/or other sight words

Materials: A group-size (6″ x 3″) set of basic sight word cards or sight words on which you want to provide practice

Procedure:

The children are divided into two teams. Each team takes a turn attempting to pronounce a word turned up from a pile of sight words. If one team misses, the opposite team then receives a chance to pronounce that word in addition to their regular turn. Score is kept on the number of words each team pronounces correctly. Do not have the members sit down when they miss a word, but have each team member go to the back of the line after each try whether successful or not. This enables all members of each team to gain equal practice and does not eliminate those people who need practice most.

Variation in Procedure:

Instead of using single or isolated words, use phrase cards or sentence cards in which the word being emphasized is underlined. Allow the children to make the cards with a final check by you. Or you can use a number of smaller teams and have several races going at one time.

Stand Up

Purpose: To provide practice on the recognition of the basic sight words and/or other sight words

Materials: Group-size word cards (6″ x 3″)

Procedure:

The children are seated in a group around you. One child stands behind the chair of another child, who is sitting with his chair facing you. You then flash a card. If the child who was standing pronounces the word before the child in the chair, then the child who was sitting must stand up behind someone else.

Word Hunt

Purpose: To provide practice on the basic sight words and/or other sight words

Materials: Blindfolds
Group-size word cards (6″ x 3″)

Procedure:

Have several children cover their eyes. The rest of the group hide the cards where they can be found easily. When all the cards are hidden those who are "it" are given a signal to immediately take off their blindfolds and begin hunting for the cards. A child may pick up a card if he knows the word on it. No cards may be taken unless the word is known. The child who finds the most words is the winner.

Seven Up

Purpose: To provide practice on word recognition and word meaning

Materials: Group-size word cards (6″ x 3″). Be sure there are seven times as many cards as children playing.

Procedure:

The children sit in a circle with flash cards which are piled facedown in the center of the group. Each child takes a turn by turning over a card and reading it. If he reads it correctly, he keeps it. When he has seven correct cards he stands up. The game continues until all the children are standing. The children then sit down and see how fast they can make a sentence with some or all of their seven cards. Be sure both nouns and verbs are included in the stack. As soon as a child has made a sentence, he stands. This play continues until all the children who can make sentences of their words have done so.

Noun Label

Purpose: To teach nouns to non-English speaking children and to improve the vocabulary of those students who are retarded in their vocabulary development. It may, of course, be used in the early stages of reading in the regular developmental program.

Materials: Group-size word cards (6″ x 3″) with the names of common nouns written on them
8½″ x 11″ tagboard sheets with a picture on one of the common nouns on the top half of the sheet

Procedure:

The pictures on the tagboard sheets are placed on the tray of the chalkboard. The children are then given words which correspond to the pictures. They come up to the chalkboard and place their words under the appropriate pictures. See the following example.

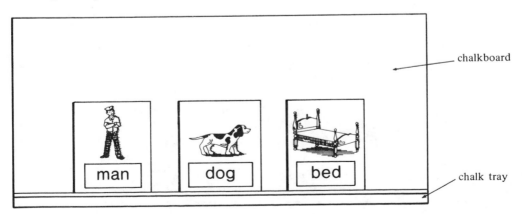

Erase Relay

Purpose: To provide practice in recognizing newly learned words

Materials: A list of words on which you wish to provide practice

Procedure:

Write on the chalkboard two columns of words that are approximately equal in difficulty. Write as many words on the board as there are children in the relay. The children then choose sides or are numbered 1, 2, 1, 2, and stand in two lines at right angles to the chalkboard. At the signal, the first child in each line points at the first word in his respective column of words and pronounces that word. If he pronounces it correctly he is allowed to erase the word. The game is won by the side that erases all the words first.

Variation in Procedure:

Do the same exercise using such sounds as long vowels, short vowels, consonants, consonant blends, prefixes, suffixes, and word parts.

Words and Pictures

Purpose: To learn and review the common nouns

Materials: Envelopes
Make word cards which are divided as shown in the following example. On one side the word should appear and on the other side there should be a picture representing that word. After the cards are completed they should be cut into two pieces. Each should be cut with a different pattern along the cut edge; however, both sides should be approximately the same size. Put about ten of these word cards and pictures (twenty pieces) inside each envelope and pass them out to the children.

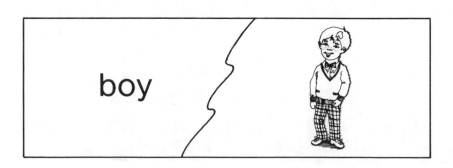

Procedure:

The children should be told to first line up the words in a column. After this is done they will pronounce the first word and check to see if it is right by putting the picture representing that word beside it. The cut edges will, of course, match if the child knew the word. If he did not know the word the game will be self correcting because he can continue to match the word and pictures until the edges do fit. Pass the envelopes around and let each child do each set.

What Is It—What Does It Mean

Purpose: To provide practice on the recognition and definitions of sight words encountered in daily reading lessons

Materials: Use lists of words which are new to the children in various reading groups. The words should be divided to indicate that Word Two came from the lesson being studied by Group Two, etc.

Procedure:

This game should be used after the children have had words introduced to them in the reading group or groups.

Choose teams from all the groups so that the children from the different groups will be used to working together. If possible, use these same groups in other school work that is not connected with reading. This way the children are not singled out in their groups but are all working together. At the time of the game, section off the two teams and start by writing a word on the board for the first child in team A. If he is in Group Three, the word would be from the story Group Three is working on. If Group One is the high group their words would be harder. The child is to pronounce the word and then use it in a sentence. If he can just pronounce it, he gets one point; if he doesn't know how to pronounce it, but can explain what it means or what it is, he gets three points. If he can do both, he gets five points. If he cannot do either, he receives no points. A word is then put on the board for team B, and so forth. A score is kept on the board so that everyone can see it. The team with the most points at the end of a designated amount of time is the winner.

Golfing

Purpose: To provide practice on the basic sight words and/or other sight words

Materials: Nine packs of word cards. Each pack should have ten sight words it it. A player and a scorekeeper

Procedure:

The player takes the first pack, shuffles them, and places them facedown in front of him. He takes a card from the top of the pack, turns it faceup, and reads it. If he misses a word, the scorekeeper makes one mark on the scoring sheet. The number incorrect for the first pack is the player's score for the first hole. He continues in this manner through the nine packs, trying to receive as small a score as possible.

What Word Am I?

Purpose: To provide practice with sight words

Materials: Two duplicate sets of cards with sight words printed on them

Procedure:

You divide the class into two groups. Each child has a word card pinned on his back. The duplicates of the cards are put on a table. The object of the game is to see which group can guess all their words first. The children take turns going to the table, picking up a word and asking, "Am I . . . ?" saying the word that is on the card he picked up. If he guesses correctly and pronounces the word correctly he keeps the card. If not, he puts the card down and takes his seat. The game continues until one group guesses all their words.

Jumping the Fence

Purpose: To provide practice on the basic sight words and other sight words

Materials: Flash cards with sight words on them
White tape

Procedure:

Place the flash cards in a row leading to the fence (white tape on the floor). A child who reads a word correctly may jump over it to reach the fence; then he can jump over it. If he misses a word, he sits down and another child has a turn.

Baseball

Purpose: To provide practice with the basic sight words, other sight words, or phonic sounds

Materials: Flash cards with basic sight words, other sight words, or phonic sounds on them

Procedure:

The four corners of the classroom may serve as bases and home plate. Two teams of players participate. One child goes to home plate. The pitcher then holds up a flash card. The child pronounces the word, defines it if possible, and uses it in a sentence. If he is correct, he advances to first base. This continues until the bases are loaded. Runs are scored as the children cross home plate. An out occurs when a child misses a word. There are three outs per team. The team with the highest score wins the game.

Variation in Procedure:

The flash cards may be vowel or consonant sounds and the child must give a word that has the same beginning or ending sound on the card.

Flinch*

Purpose: This game is adaptable and may be varied to reinforce many reading skills, but it is especially valuable in developing vocabulary in the content areas. This game works well with two to four players and may be played with as many as six.

Materials: The deck is composed of fifty-two cards numbered from 0–12. In each deck there will be four cards numbered *0*, four numbered *1*, four numbered *2*, etc. On another part of the card there will be a word. Use terms or words peculiar to the unit and any other words in the basal text which are new or difficult.

Procedure:

The dealer shuffles and deals out all of the cards one at a time. Each player stacks his cards facedown in front of him. The first player to the left of the dealer draws off his top card, pronounces the word, and places the card faceup beside his original stack. Should the player fail to pronounce the word, his opponents help him and then the word is placed on the bottom of the original stack to be redrawn at a later time. Play rotates to the left, each player turning up a card and playing it on an opponent's pile if he can find a place where the card will play. Zero cards play on any opponent's card pile. Number 1 cards are played in a pot in the middle of a table. The first player to turn over a Number 1 card begins the pot or center pile. Any other number card plays only if it is an adjacent number to one showing on an opponent's pile: e.g., a 7 card would play on either a 6 or 8 card. Should a player fail to see a play, any opponent may call it and then each player in turn gives the person overlooking his play an extra card which is placed on the bottom of his

---

* Invented by Mrs. Alice Hays of Imperial, Nebraska.

original stack. The game ends when one player disposes of all the cards in his original stack.

The Witch

Purpose: To provide practice with sight words. This game works well with four players if twenty cards are used.

Materials: Use a deck containing about twenty cards with one additional card which has a witch on it. Print one word on half of the cards. Duplicate the first set of words on the other half of the cards.

Procedure:

One person deals out all the cards and all players then pick them up. Beginning with the person at the dealer's left, the players take turns drawing cards. Each player draws from the person on his right. As pairs are formed, the words are pronounced and the pair is placed on the table. This play continues until all cards are matched. The player left with the witch is the loser and receives a *w*. The next time he loses he is a *wi,* etc. The object is to try to avoid losing enough times to spell *witch.*

Word-Object Hunt

Purpose: To teach and/or reinforce words used as nouns

Materials: A number of flash cards with the names of various objects written on them

Procedure:

Each student is given about twelve cards which he spreads out before him. You then say, "I went to the grocery store to buy b_____." Any student may raise his hand if he has an object which starts with *b* and would normally be bought at a grocery store. You then verify the answer and all students get a chance to look at the word. The game may be varied by not giving the beginning letter and by using the names of objects bought in various stores.

Silly Sentences

Purpose: To teach and/or reinforce sight words

Materials: Plain cardboard flash cards and/or flash cards with flannel backing and a flannel board.

Procedure:

Either lay out sentences in mixed-up order on a table or on a flannel board. Have students take turns coming up and unscrambling the sentences and reading them after they are placed in a sensible order. Make sure all students get a chance to read each logically ordered sentence.

Tape-Recorded Object Search

Purpose: To teach and/or reinforce sight words

Materials: Tape recorder
Cassettes
Envelopes
Sight word cards

Procedure:

Tape-record a message which says, "Lay all of your cards out in front of you in two rows. There are eight cards. Place four cards in the top row and four cards in the bottom row. Turn the tape recorder off until you have done this." (Allow a four second pause.) "Listen carefully. We need a scale to weigh the package. Pick up the word *scale*." (Allow about five seconds per word.) "The word *scale* has a number four on the back of it. Check to see if you got it right." When playing this game make sure each card is numbered 1–8 so that they can easily be checked. Place a tape cassette and eight cards in each envelope. Number the envelopes and give students sheets with corresponding numbers on them so they can check off each envelope after it has been completed.

Matching Nouns and Verbs

Purpose: To teach and/or reinforce sight words

Materials: Envelopes
Sight word cards

Procedure:

In each envelope place about ten nouns and ten verbs. Have them read as follows:

birds	fly
brooms	sweep
people	talk

Instruct students to match the noun with the proper verb. Number the correct pairs with matching numbers so that the students can check the pairs on their own. Number the envelopes and give students sheets with corresponding numbers so that they can check off each envelope after it has been completed.

Matching Noun Pictures with Words

Purpose: To teach various noun sight words

Materials: Pictures cut from catalogs and other sources
             Small cards
             Envelopes

Procedure:

Place about fifteen or twenty pictures in each envelope and the name of the object in the picture on a small card. On the back of the card and matching picture write a number so that each match. Also number each envelope. Pass out envelopes to students and instruct them to match the pictures with their written names.When they are done they can look at the numbers on the back of each card and pictures to make sure they have matched them correctly. Give students a sheet of paper with as many numbers on it as you have envelopes. When they complete each envelope they should check it off their numbered sheet. This will insure that each student does each envelope.

11. Guesses at Words

RECOGNIZED BY

Pupil guesses at new words instead of analyzing the correct pronunciation.

DISCUSSION

Guessing at words may be the result of one or several factors. The pupil simply may not possess a knowledge of phonics or structural analysis. He may not know how to systematically sound out a word, or he may not be using context clues. Before attempting to help the pupil, you should determine which of the factors are responsible for the pupil's guessing at words. A very effective way of determining why a pupil guesses at words is simply to *ask him*. You should ask whether he knows the sound of the first letter, the blend, the vowel combinations, the first syllable, and so forth. Also, you should check to see whether the student knows how to blend sounds together rapidly. Finally, ask questions to determine whether he is aware of the context in which the word is used. If it is determined that the pupil has no knowledge of phonics and/or structural analysis, the suggestion listed under Item (A) should be followed. If he has knowledge of phonics, but doesn't use it, then the suggestion listed under Item (B) will be helpful. Pupils who do not make use of the context should be given help as recommended in items (C), (D), (E), and (F).

RECOMMENDATIONS

A.   Administer the *El Paso Phonics Survey**, the *CRS (Phonics Section)* † or a similar test that examines a situation that approximates what the student would have to do if actually reading in your classroom. Give help where needed according to the results of the test. Recommendations for correcting difficulties in the areas of phonics and structural analysis are found in the following sections:

---

* Eldon E. Ekwall, *A Teacher's Handbook in Diagnosis and Remediation in Reading* (Boston: Allyn and Bacon, Longwood Division, 1977), Chapter 5.

† Eldon E. Ekwall, "Phonics," *Corrective Reading System* (Glenview, Illinois: Psychotechnics, Inc., 1976).

Phonics—Sections 12, p. 57; 13, p. 67; and 14, p. 73.
Structural Analysis—Section 15, p. 75.

B.   While the child is reading orally, the teacher should call attention to the words at which the reader guesses. At the same time help should be given in the systematic analysis of the word. This will start the reader into the habit of analyzing his own difficult words. Help him to sound the first sound, the second, and on through to the end of the word. Then give help in blending these sounds together.

C.   As the pupil reads, circle or underline the words he guesses. Present the material read by the pupil to him in a form in which the words he guesses are blank lines. Ask him to fill in the correct words from context.

D.   Try to develop the habit of having the pupil re-read several words preceding the difficult word and sound out at least the first one or two sounds of the difficult word. Then read several words following the difficult word. This strategy will develop the habit of using context as well as the beginning sounds. The pupil will learn to sound more of the word than the first syllable as the need arises. For example: "The large black dog was ch_____ on the bone." If the pupil has read *on the bone* and hears the sound of *ch,* he will in most cases say *chewing.*

E.   Give the pupil sentences in which there is one difficult word which he has guessed in his oral reading. Have him work independently, using the method described in (C) to determine correctness of the difficult words.

F.   Teach the pupil that there are a number of types of context clues. He does not have to categorize them; however, working with several different kinds will enable him to become more adept in their use. For example:

1.   Definition context clues:
The word *mongrel* sometimes refers to a *dog* of mixed breeds.

2.   Synonym context clues:
The team was *gleeful* and the coach was also *jubliant* because they had won the game.

3.   Contrasting words:
He was *antisocial,* but she was *friendly.*

4.   Common sayings or expressions:
It was *dark* as *pitch.*

G.   Use commercially prepared materials designed to improve use of context clues. (See Appendix B.)

12. Consonant Sounds Unknown

RECOGNIZED BY

Pupil is unable to give the correct sounds and variant sounds of the consonants. (See Appendix A.)

DISCUSSION

Some phonic systems teach the consonants prior to teaching the vowels, while others teach the vowels before the consonants. However, the pupil must know both his consonant and vowel sounds, variant consonant and vowel sounds, as well as common blends. (See Appendix A.) Before beginning a program of help in phonics, administer the *El Paso Phonics Survey,* the *CRS (Phonics Section),* or some similar test that requires the student to respond as he would in actually reading. Group tests will simply not do this. You can then base help on the weaknesses indicated by the test. A test of this nature will not only tell you whether or not the pupil knows the various sounds, but it will also tell you whether the pupil knows the sounds but does not know how to use them.

RECOMMENDATIONS

A. Construct flash cards in which the consonant is shown along with a picture illustrating a word which uses that consonant: e.g., *b* in *b*all, and *c* in *c*at. On the opposite side of the flash card print the letter only. This can be used as the pupil progresses in ability. See example following.

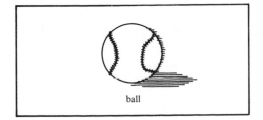

ball

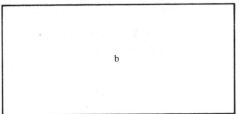

b

Front of Card   Back of Card

B.   Put the consonant letters on cards (3″ x 3″). Divide these cards into groups of ten each. Lay out separate groups of letters so that the pupil can see all ten at once. As you call the sounds of letters, or as they are played from a tape recording, have the pupil pick up the correct card to match the sound of the letter. As there are fewer words to observe—that is, after some have already been picked up—you will need to speed up the rate at which you pronounce the remaining words. The following timing seems to work well: pronounce the first word, wait 7 seconds; pronounce the second word and wait 7 seconds again; then 6, 6, 5, 5, 4, 4, and 3. Many students are unable to manipulate the cards in less time than this.

C.   Tape-record words and have the children write the letter they hear at the beginning and/or end of these words. See the following example.

Directions: As you hear a word called on the tape, write the letter that begins the word. (Tape script says, "Number One is *come*, Number Two is *dog*," etc.)

1.   c
2.   d
3.
4.
5.

D.   Use the same system as in (C). Instead of having the pupils write letters they hear, have them pick up the card matching the beginning or ending letter they hear in the words.

E.   Put various consonant letters on the board and have the children make lists of the words which begin with these letters.

F.   Record the consonant letters with their sounds and let the students hear these as many times as it is necessary to learn them. They should, however, have a chart which they can follow to see the letters as they hear the sound.

G.   Use commercial charts which are available for teaching consonants. Records that give the proper pronunciation of the consonant sounds are also available. (See Appendix B.)

H.   Use commercially prepared games designed to teach consonants and consonant usage. (See Appendix B.)

GAMES AND EXERCISES

Phonic Rummy

Purpose: To provide practice in various phonic elements. This game works well with two to four players when using 36 cards, or up to six players when using 48 or 52 cards.

Materials: A deck of cards with phonic elements that you wish to teach. On each card will appear one phonic element and four words which use that particular phonic element. One of the four words will be underlined. The deck may consist of 36, 40, 44, 48 or 52 cards. For each phonic element there will be four cards, each of which has a different word underlined. A deck of 36 cards would involve nine phonic elements; 40 cards would involve ten phonic elements. See the following example of the cards:

i	*ay*	*gr*
did	stay	green
pit	may	grass
if	play	grow
fish	clay	grab

Procedure:

The dealer shuffles the cards and deals eight cards, facedown, to each player. The rest of the cards are placed facedown in the center of the table. The first player to the left of the dealer calls for a word using a certain phonic element on which he wishes to build. (See the examples.) For example, he might say, "I want Sam to give me *fish* from the *i* group." He would pronounce the short *i* sound. If Sam had that card he would give it to the caller. The player (caller) then continues to call for certain cards from specific people. If the person called upon does not have the card, the player takes a card from the center pile and the next player to the left takes his turn. When a player completes a "book" (i.e. he has all four cards from a certain phonic element) he lays it down. Players can only lay down "books" when it is their turn to draw. The object is to get the most books before someone empties his hand.

Think

Purpose: To provide practice with initial vowels, consonants, and initial consonant blends. This game works well with four players.

Materials: Enough small cards so that each letter of the alphabet and all the initial blends can be printed on a separate card. There may be more than one card for each vowel.

Procedure:

Place the cards facedown on the table. The players take turns selecting a card and naming a word which begins with the same letter or blend. If someone cannot name a word within five seconds, he puts the card back. The winner is the person who has the greatest number of cards after the entire pile has been drawn.

Checkers

Purpose: To provide practice on various vowel and/or consonant sounds, and to improve auditory discrimination

Materials: Cards with phonic elements such as consonant sounds, vowel digraphs, and diphthongs on them
Large squares of paper in two contrasting colors

Procedure:

Draw a checkerboard on the floor or place sheets of construction paper on the floor in a checkerboard pattern. Divide the children into two groups and place each group back to back on the two middle rows. Each group must not have more children in it than there are squares across one row of the checkerboard. Each child stands on a square and holds one card with a sound on it. You either call a word or have the word pre-recorded on the tape recorder, which has the sound that corresponds with the sound on the card the child holds. When a child hears a word that has his sound in it he may move one square toward the outer part of the checkerboard. The object of the game is for one side to reach the king row first. If a child misses a sound, or moves when he should not then his side has to move a player back one space. There may be times when several children will move at once depending, of course, on the words chosen by you.

Variation in Procedure:

Play the same game, but ask comprehension questions over a reading assignment that all the children have read.

Word Trail

Purpose: To provide practice on consonants, consonant blends, vowels, digraphs and diphthongs

Materials: A piece of tagboard
A list of phonic elements to be taught
A die

Procedure:

Draw a margin (approximately two inches) around the sheet of tagboard. Divide the margin into spaces large enough for inserting the phonic elements for practice. On the corners and in several spaces between corners insert penalties and rewards such as, "Take another turn"; "Move back three spaces." The players then take turns shaking the die and moving their players (perhaps pieces of corn) along the spaces, saying each phonic element as they move. If they cannot say a certain phonic element they must stop on the space behind it and wait for another turn. The first player around the "word trail" is the winner.

Any Card

Purpose: To provide practice with consonants, consonant digraphs, consonant blends, and rhyming sounds. This game can be played with two to four players.

Materials: A deck of thirty-six to fifty-two cards with words such as the following:

pan	fun	sock	mill	call	harm
man	bun	knock	still	fall	charm
can	run	shock	kill	ball	farm

Also include four cards with *any card* written on them.

Procedure:

A player deals out five cards. The player to the left of the dealer plays any one of his cards, naming it as it is played. The next player plays a card that either rhymes or begins with the same letter as the first card. For example, if *sun* has been played, *bun* rhyming with *sun* or *sock* with the same first letter could be played. If a child cannot play, he draws from the pile in the center until he can play or has drawn three times. If he has the card with *any card* written on it, he may play this card and name a word that can be played upon it. The first player who runs out of cards wins the game.

I'm Thinking of a Word

Purpose: To provide practice in auditory discrimination and the recognition of beginning and/or ending sounds

Materials: Pocket chart
            Cards with words that begin with various consonants
            Cards that end with various consonants

Procedure:

Fill the pocket chart with about ten cards, each of which has a different beginning sound. The first child may say, "I'm thinking of a word that begins like *d* [sound of *d*]." One child continues to try to find cards until he misses one. The object is to get all the cards.

Variation in Procedure:

There are many possible variations of this game. You may have children come up to the front and say, "I'm thinking . . .", etc., and call on someone to guess the word. A child may put letters in the pocket chart and say, "My word is *dog*." The other children then have to find a *d* or *g* depending on whether you are working with beginning or ending sounds. The children also may play the same game and be required to find both the beginning and ending sounds.

Catch the Stick

Purpose: To improve auditory discrimination and to improve the children's ability to make the connection between sounds and letters

Materials: A number of group-size cards (6″ x 3″) with the beginning consonant sounds on them
            A yardstick

Procedure:

Seat the children in as small a circle as possible for the number of children you wish to have play the game. Ten to twelve children are optimum. The children are all given a different beginning consonant sound on a group-size card. One child stands in the center of the circle and holds a yardstick in an upright position with one end on the floor and the top end held in place by the tip of his finger. The child in the center then pronounces a word that begins with a consonant. At the same time he pronounces the word, he takes the tip of his finger off the top of the yardstick. The child who has the beginning letter of the word given by the child in the center of the circle must catch the yardstick before it falls on the floor. If the child who had the consonant letter catches the stick, he takes his seat again and the person in the center must say another word. If he does not, then he must hold the stick. The child in the center then takes the card held by the child who took his place.

Blending Wheel

Purpose: To provide practice on blending beginning and ending consonants and consonant blends

Materials: Two cardboard circles, one of which is approximately two inches smaller in diameter (a convenient size is 8″ and 10″)

Procedure:

Fasten the two circles together with a paper fastener as shown in the following illustration. The outside circle should have word roots or major parts of a word on it, and the inside circle should have a specific consonant or consonant blend on which you wish to provide practice. Have the child rotate one of the circles and practice blending the root or word part with the blend.

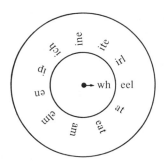

Word Puzzles

Purpose: To provide practice in recognizing blend sounds and to provide practice in blending

Materials: Envelopes
Word cards

Procedure:

Cut a few word cards of equal size. Print a word containing a blend which has been taught: eg., *gl*ad, *st*and, on each card. Cut each word in two between the blend and the remainder of the word. Place about eight to ten of these in each envelope and pass out the envelopes to the children. The children then assemble the blends and word parts to make words. After being checked by you, the envelopes are exchanged so that each child eventually assembles the words in each enevlope.

Phonics Posters

Purpose: To develop an awareness of related sounds

Materials: Tagboard
Old magazines or old textbooks

Procedure:

At the top of a piece of tagboard place a letter or combination of letters. Have the children find pictures of objects in magazines or old readers that start with the sound or sounds displayed in the heading. These object pictures should be cut out and mounted on the tagboard to provide practice for the individuals who need special help.

Poet Play

Purpose: To help children develop an awareness of sound similarities through the use of rhyming words

Materials: Pocket chart
           Word cards
           Envelopes

Procedure:

Give the children envelopes containing a number of word cards. Place a master word in the pocket chart and have the children locate in their envelopes a word that rhymes with the one posted. Number the envelopes and allow the children to exchange them after each round so that they will become familiar with a great many words and their sound similarities.

Stand-Up

Purpose: To provide practice in discriminating between like and unlike sounds

Procedure:

When there is extra time before lunch or dismissal, you might use this game. It is both interesting and beneficial. You call, "All those whose names start like *meat* may stand up and get their coats." Repeat as many times as needed to dismiss the children. As a variation, use letters that are in the middle or end of children's names. The children also might use this same method to choose groups or sides in other games.

Rhyme Time

Purpose: To discover which children are having auditory discrimination problems and to provide practice through the use of related phonic sounds

Materials: Tagboard
           Word cards

Procedure:

Write sentences on the tagboard. On small word cards print a variety of words which will rhyme with selected words given in the sentences. Have the children locate and match their cards with the rhyming words in the sentences. Place each set of cards in an envelope and number the envelopes so that the children can keep a record of the sets on which they have worked. See the example following.

1. The <u>dog</u> bit the mailperson. (log, hog, etc.)

2. The candy tasted <u>sweet</u>. (treat, beat)

3. <u>Look</u> out the window. (took, book)

4. The wall had a large <u>crack</u>. (back, sack)

5. He cut down the apple <u>tree</u>. (see, flee)

Making and Exchanging Picture Dictionaries

Purpose: To learn initial consonant sounds

Materials: Old notebooks or paper to be bound together
             Crayons and/or paints
             Magazines and other materials containing pictures

Procedure:

Have students cut out or draw pictures representing various initial consonant sounds. Under the picture write the letter(s) and the word that stands for the picture. Also under each picture use the word in a sentence. After the students have finished their books have them exchange dictionaries so that each student learns to read every other student's dictionary.

Hard and Soft *C* and *G*

Purpose: To teach the rules for hard and soft *c* and *g*

Materials: Rule chart with pockets and flash cards with various *c* or *g* words on them

Procedure:

Construct a large chart about 8½" x 11" like the chart on page 66. The bottom half should contain two large pockets marked as shown. The top half should contain the rule for soft and hard *c* or *g*. Students are then given a number of flash cards with soft and hard *g* words on them. They put each card into the appropriate pocket according to the rule stated on the chart. Students may check their own work if the words *hard* or *soft* are written on the back of each flash card. (Do the same for *c*.)

G followed by *e, i,* or *y* usually has a soft sound.

If *g* is followed by any other letter, it usually has a hard sound.

Hard *g*	Soft *g*
(*game*)	(gentle)

13. Vowel Sounds Not Known

RECOGNIZED BY

Pupil is unable to give the correct sounds and variant sounds of the vowels. (See Appendix A.)

DISCUSSION

In the past there have been many rules that supposedly should be learned by students who are learning phonics as an aid to word attack skills. However, research studies over the past ten years have shown that some of the rules formerly taught have little utility in reading programs. Rules which appear to be worthwhile teaching are as follows:

1. If there is only one vowel letter and it appears at the end of a word, the letter usually has a long sound. Note that this is only true for one syllable words.
2. A single vowel in a syllable usually has a short sound if it is not the last letter in a syllable or is not followed by r.
3. A vowel followed by r usually has a sound that is neither long nor short.
4. When y is preceded by a consonant in a one syllable word, the y usually has the sound of long i; but in words of two or more syllables the final y usually has the sound of long e. Some people hear it as short i.
5. In words ending in vowel-consonant e the e is silent and the vowel may be either long or short. Try the long sound first.
6. When ai, ay, ea, ee, and oa are found together, the first vowel is usually long and the second is silent.
7. The vowel pair ow may have either the long o sound as in low or the ou sound as in owl.
8. When au, aw, ou, oi, and oy are found together, they usually blend or form a diphthong.
9. The oo sound is either long as in moon or short as in book.
10. If a is the only vowel in a syllable and it is followed by l or w, then the a will usually be neither long nor short, but will have the awe sound heard in ball and awl.

These rules certainly do not cover all the rules or exceptions; however, learning too many rules often proves almost as fruitless as knowing none. Furthermore, a student who has passed the primary grades (first, second, and third) will often find it difficult to learn by the use of rules. You should not attempt to give a great deal of remediation until you are fairly sure what areas of phonics are causing difficulty for the pupil. The *El Paso Phonics Survey* or the *CRS (Phonics Section)* will help to determine where the student is weak. You should administer one of them to determine whether the student knows his vowel sounds, vowel rules, and so on. The tests will not only help determine whether the student knows the sounds and rules, but also show whether he is able to apply them in the analysis of a word. Remember that some reading programs do not teach the vowel sounds until the student is in the second grade. Some students do not possess adequate auditory discrimination abilities to deal with these sounds until this time. A few, of course, have problems in discrimination of sounds far beyond the second grade.

RECOMMENDATIONS

A. Construct flash cards in which the vowel is shown along with a picture illustrating a word which uses that vowel, e.g., short *a* in hat, long *a* in rake. On the opposite side print only the vowel letter marked long or short to be used as the pupil progresses in ability. When using this method with an entire class, 2″ x 2″ slides or transparencies for the overhead projector can be substituted for flash cards. For example:

Front of Card   Back of Card

B. Have the children circle or underline the words in a line which have vowels with the same sound as the first word in the line. See the following examples.

1. Long—lone - dog - of - to
2. Rat—car - bear - happy - same
3. Line—with - win - wild - is
4. Treat—tread - same - easy - well

C. Record the vowel letters with their sounds and variant sounds and play them to the students as many times as it is necessary to learn them. They should, however, have a chart which they can follow to see the letter as they hear the sound.

D. Put the vowel letters on cards (3″ x 3″). Use the breve (˘) or the macron (−) to indicate the short and long sounds. Divide these cards into groups of ten each. Lay out separate groups of letters so that the pupil can see ten at once. As you call the sounds of the vowel letters, or as they are played from a tape recording, have the pupil pick up the correct card to match the sound of the letter. [See directions under (B) for "Consonant Sounds Not Known," Section 12, page 58.]

E. Use the same system as in (D). Instead of having the children match letters they hear, have them write the letter matching the letter sound they hear in the words.

F. Use commercial charts which are available for teaching vowels. Records to accompany the sounds are also available. (See Appendix B.)

G. Use commercially prepared games designed for teaching the vowels and vowel usage. (See Appendix B.)

GAMES AND EXERCISES

Game Board for Sorting Vowel Sounds

Purpose: To learn to hear various vowel sounds

Materials: Picture and/or words with various vowel sounds in them.
Construct a board as follows:

	A	E	I	O	U
Long					
Short					
R = Controlled					

Procedure:

Have students sort pictures and/or words into the correct intersecting squares (pictures must be used with beginning readers) according to the sound in the name of the object in the picture. For example, *hen* would go under the square under the *e* column and the row across from *short*. The pictures from some commercially sold games such as *Vowel Lotto* work well with this game board.

Vowel Tic-tac-toe

Purpose: To learn vowel sounds

Materials: Flash cards with the following written on them:

Short *a*	Long *a*	R-controlled *a*
Short *e*	Long *e*	R-controlled *e*
Short *i*	Long *i*	R-controlled *i*
Short *o*	Long *o*	R-controlled *o*
Short *u*	Long *u*	R-controlled *u*

Procedure:

Have two students play tic-tac-toe. However, instead of marking each square with *X* or *O* have them each draw a card before the game starts. If, for example, one student gets short *o* and the other gets long *a*, then each person must write a word with that sound when it is his turn to play instead of making the traditional *X* or *O*. An example of a partially finished game is shown below:

cake		
	hot	
make		pot

Variation in Procedure:

This is also a good learning device if the two participants have to draw a new card before each move. When playing the game this way, use two different colors of chalk or pencil to help remember which words belong to each player.

Sorting Pictures According to Matching Vowel Sounds

Purpose: To teach short and long vowel sounds

Materials: Construct a large chart using all of the short and long vowel sounds on pictures placed on pockets as shown below. On the top half of the chart, glue a large envelope in place. Find many pictures representing various short and long vowel sounds and place them in the large envelope.

Procedure:

Construct the chart similar to the example.

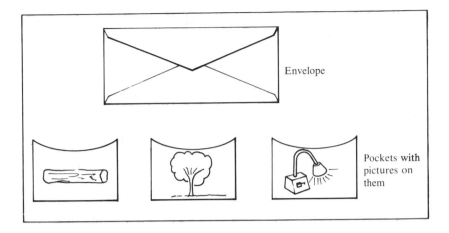

Envelope

Pockets with pictures on them

NOTE: This illustration shows only three pictures, a log, tree, and light. There should, of course, be *ten* pictures, each representing a short or long vowel sound.

Have students take pictures from the large envelope and say the word related to the picture. Remind them to listen for the vowel sound they hear in that word. Then have them find the corresponding vowel sound from the picture on the pockets below and place the picture from the large envelope in the proper pocket. This activity can be made self-checking by numbering the backs of the pictures from the large envelope to correspond with the small pocket it should go in; i.e., after students have placed all of the pictures from the large envelope in the small pockets, they can merely turn the pictures over to see if they match the numbers on the small pockets.

Sorting Vowel Sounds

Purpose: To learn to hear various vowel sounds

Materials: Ten shoe boxes for each group
             About 100 word cards, each using the sound of only one vowel

Procedure:

You or a team captain draws a card. Students read it and listen for a specific vowel sound. They then analyze the word and place it into the correctly marked short or long *a, e, i, o,* or *u* shoe box.

Vowel Relay

Purpose: To give practice in blending and learning sight words

Materials: Flash cards with various vowel sounds written on them such as the following:

Long *a*	Short *a*	R-controlled *a*	L-controlled *a*
Long *e*	Short *e*	R-controlled *e*	W-controlled *a*
Long *i*	Short *i*	R-controlled *i*	W-controlled *o*
Long *o*	Short *o*	R-controlled *o*	W-controlled *e*
Long *u*	Short *u*	R-controlled *u*	

Procedure:

Divide the students into two groups and the chalkboard into two parts. Each group lines up in front of their half of the chalkboard. The pile of cards are divided in half and placed in the chalk tray below each of the two divisions of the chalkboard. You say "Go," at which time the two front players each move up and turn over a card. Each player must write a word using his designated vowel sound in a period of ten seconds. However, a new player cannot move up until you again say "Go" in ten seconds. If he fails, he merely draws a line and the next player moves up and turns over another card and does the same when you say "Go." The team who has all of their cards turned over with the most correct words is the winner.

NOTE: Much of the material listed under "Games and Exercises" in Section 12, p. 57, can be adapted for teaching the vowel sounds.

14. Blends, Digraphs, or Diphthongs Not Known

RECOGNIZED BY

Pupil is unable to give the correct sounds of the blends, digraphs, and diphthongs.

DISCUSSION

As with the consonant and vowel sounds, it is essential that the pupil know the blends, diagraphs, and diphthong sounds in order to analyze certain words. The *El Paso Phonics Survey* or the *CRS (Phonics Section)* will help you determine which areas are causing the most difficulty for the pupil. It also will help you to determine whether the pupil possesses a knowledge of the blends, and/or digraphs and diphthong sounds but does not use his knowledge. The test should be administered before beginning a program of help in this area.

RECOMMENDATIONS

A. Construct flash cards in which the blend, digraph, or diphthong is shown along with a picture illustrating a word using that letter combination. See Appendix A for suggested words. On the opposite side of the card print only the blend, digraph, or diphthong to be used as the pupil progresses in ability. When using this method with an entire class, 2″ x 2″ slides or transparencies for the overhead projector can be substituted for the flash cards. [See illustration of card under (A), "Vowel Sounds Not Known," Section 13, p. 68].

B. Record the letter combinations with their sounds and let the students hear these as many times as it is necessary to learn them. They should, however, have a chart which they can follow to see the letter combinations as they hear the sounds. Ask each pupil to point to the letters as he hears them on the tape.

C. Put diphthongs, digraphs, and blends on cards (3″ x 3″). Divide these cards into groups of ten each. Lay out separate groups of diphthongs, digraphs, and blends, allowing the pupil to see all ten at once. As you call the sounds of these various letter combinations or as they are played from a tape recording, have the pupil pick up the correct card to match the sound of the letter combinations. [See directions under (B), "Consonant Sounds Not Known," Section 12, p. 58].

D.   Use the same system mentioned in (C), only tape-record words and have the pupil pick up the letter combinations he hears in these words.

E.   Use commercial charts that are available for teaching various letter combinations. Recordings to accompany these sounds are also available. (See Appendix B.)

F.   Use commercially prepared games that the children can play individually or in groups. (See Appendix B.)

GAMES AND EXERCISES

See "Games and Exercises," "Improving Ability in Phonics," Section 12, p. 58, and "Games and Exercises," Section 13, p. 69. Much of the material listed under these two categories can be adapted to the teaching of blends, digraphs, and diphthongs.

15. Lacks Desirable Structural Analysis

RECOGNIZED BY

Pupil is unable to gain clues to the pronunciation of a word or its meaning by finding familiar elements of that word within the word. (See definition of structural analysis, page 4.)

DISCUSSION

Structural analysis begins when the child is able to recognize the root word in words with *s*, *ed*, etc., endings: e.g., *run* in *run*s, and *look* in *look*ed. From this beginning, he should learn to recognize the parts which make up compound words, such as *tooth* and *ache* in *toothache,* and *green* and *house* in *greenhouse*. He also may begin to recognize common roots, suffixes, prefixes, and important letter groups such as *tion*. Some authorities in the field of reading feel that it is not good, however, to look for little words within bigger words, as they may not have their usual pronunciation. The child should learn the principles of syllabication which will enable him to divide words into pronounceable units.

One of the best ways to determine whether a student is having difficulty with structural analysis is to ask him to read orally. While he reads orally you can note the types of errors he makes and can also ask questions to ascertain whether he knows certain root words, ending sounds, beginning sounds, word families, parts of compound words, contractions, and affixes. Teachers who are familiar with components of structural analysis will usually find a definite pattern of mistakes within a certain area or overlapping into several areas.

RECOMMENDATIONS

A. Make lists of the common word endings and have the children underline these endings and pronounce their sounds.

B. Use multiple choice questions which require the pupil to put the proper endings on words. See examples following.

1. The boy was (looked, looks, looking) in the window.

2. That is (John, John's, Johns) ball and bat.

    3.   The boys came (early, earlier, earliest) than the girls.

C.   Make lists or flash cards of the common roots, prefixes, and suffixes. Use these in forming new words. You may have a drill on these sounds, but should not require memorization of the meanings of affixes. (See Appendix G for list of suffixes and prefixes.)

D.   Make lists or flash cards of common letter combinations such as *tion* and *ult*. A drill on these may be very helpful; however, try to avoid listing letter combinations which have sounds that may vary according to the word in which they are used. Lists may be made on transparencies for the overhead projector or on large pieces of cardboard.

E.   Make lists of and discuss compounds words as the pupil encounters them in his reading lessons.

F.   Make lists of all the words that can be made from certain roots. For example:

    1.   work—works, working, worked

    2.   carry—carrying, carrier, carried, carries

    3.   faith—faithful, faithless

    4.   lodge—lodger, lodging, lodged, lodgment

G.   Write a number of words on the board with prefixes that mean the same thing, e.g., *imperfect, untied, irreplaceable.* Have the pupils add to the list. Underline roots and/or prefixes and discuss them.

H.   Make a list of words to which the pupil adds prefixes or suffixes to give a certain meaning to the word. For example:

Directions: Add a suffix to make these words mean *one who does* or *that which does*:

work	extract
elevate	pretend
play	repel
contract	admires

I.   Construct drills in which the pupil may learn words by filling in blanks according to the proper context. For example:

    1.   *Hydroelectric* refers to the production of electricity by the use of water.

    2.   Something which existed before is preexistent.

J.   Teach the pupil the syllabication principles and work through a number of words to enable him to become very proficient at dividing words into syllables. The main syllabication principles follow.

1. When two consonants stand between two vowels the word is usually divided between the consonants: e.g., *dag-ger* and *cir-cus.*

2. When one consonant stands between two vowels, the consonant usually goes with the second syllable unless the vowel on the right is a final *e,* in which case there is no syllable division: e.g., *mo-tor, pa-per,* and *receive.*

3. When a word ends in a consonant and *le,* the consonont usually begins the last syllable: *ca-ble.*

4. Compound words are usually divided between the word parts and between syllables within these parts: *tooth-ache, mas-ter-mind.*

5. In most cases, do not divide between the letters in consonant digraphs or consonant blends. (See Appendix A for lists of consonant digraphs and consonant blends.)

6. Prefixes and suffixes are usually separate syllables. Examples: *dis-own, north-ward.* Use Appendix G as a study aid to help pupils recognize prefixes and suffixes.

GAMES AND EXERCISES

Prefix and Suffix Baseball

Purpose: To provide practice in recognizing prefixes, suffixes and their meanings

Materials: Make cards with a prefix such as *un____* or a suffix such as *____ly* on them. Be sure to include the line to indicate whether it is a prefix or a suffix.

Procedure:

This game is not to be used until considerable work has been done with prefixes and suffixes. English-speaking children have less trouble with it since they already have a large vocabulary and only need to realize that these words contain prefixes and suffixes.

Each of the two teams chooses a pitcher who will dig a box and "pitch" a word to the "batter." The batter will think of a word to go with the prefix or suffix and then pronounce it. If he does this much but cannot use it in a sentence, he has made a "single." If he can think of a word, pronounce it, and use it in a sentence, he hits a "double." After the children become more adept at the game, you may wish to confine the hits to singles to slow down the game.

Caution! Remember that only a few suffix and prefix meanings are consistent enough to warrant memorizing their meanings.

Dig Up the Root

Purpose: To develop recognition of word roots and attached affixes

Materials: Pocket chart
            Word cards

Procedure:

Divide the pocket chart into two columns. On the left-hand side, list a number of root words. In an adjacent column, randomly list words composed of the root words plus an affix. Have the children match the root word in the first one with the root and its affix in the second column.

1.	finish	undecided
2.	reach	finishing
3.	determine	replace
4.	decided	nationality
5.	place	reached
6.	nation	predetermine

Prefix and Suffix Chart

Purpose: To teach the meanings and uses of suffixes and prefixes

Materials: Exercises constructed by you similar to the following example

Procedure:

Construct a chart like the following and have the students fill in the blank spaces. Place an X in the spaces that are not applicable.

Prefix	Prefix Meaning	Root	Whole Word	Suffix	Suffix Meaning
un	—	do	undo	x	x
x	x	soft	softly	—	in a way
x	x	play	playful	ful	—
—	from	Port	—	x	x
Pre	—	—	—	x	x
x	x	care	—	—	without
re	—	gain	—	x	x

Spinning for Suffixes
(For small groups of 2–5 people)

Purpose: To give practice in recognizing and attaching suffixes. Also this game will help the pupil to learn the meanings of certain suffixes.

Materials: A heavy piece of cardboard or a piece of plywood cut in a circle about two to three feet in diameter. Around the edge of the board write a few suffixes so that they occupy the same positions as the numbers on the face of a clock. See example.
Extra overlays of paper to attach to the face of the circle. These overlays will enable you to readily change the suffixes with which you are working.
A pointer in the center of the circle so that it can be spun.
A number of word cards that can be used with each overlay. For example, for the prefixes *ed, ing,* and *tion* on the overlay you might use the word *direct* on a word card.

Procedure:

Pass out an equal number of word cards to each member of the group. You or a student then spins the pointer which stops on a certain suffix. You call on each member of the group, asking them to take their top card and try to attach the suffix at which the pointer stopped. The children may be asked to spell and pronounce the word, and then define what it means. When a child has done this correctly, he puts his card in a box. The child who has all his cards in the box first is the winner.

Variation in Procedure:

Make overlays that contain prefixes to fit in the face of the circle and play the game in the same manner as was done with the suffixes.

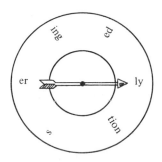

Send Over

Purpose: To provide practice in structural analysis by adding various endings to verbs

Materials: Large cards with a verb printed on each of them

Procedure:

Two teams are formed by any method the students may wish. Each team is given half the cards. When the first team holds up one of its cards and says "send (name of person) over," that person must then say four forms of the verb correctly. If he is correct, he chooses one member of the other team to be on his side. If he is incorrect, he must go over to the opposing team. The game ends when the teams run out of verbs or when all players are on one team.

Go Fish

Purpose: To provide practice in structural analysis

Materials: A deck of cards, approximately the same size as regular playing cards. Each card should have a particular form of a verb printed on it: e.g., *jump, jumps, jumped, jumping.* There should be four cards in each book and as many books as desired. A book consists of the four forms of a verb.

Procedure:

Each player is dealt four cards. The remainder of the pack is placed face down in the center of the table. Each player in turn asks another player for a card to complete his book. If he receives the card, he may ask again. He may continue to ask as long as he receives the card he is asking for. If the person does not have the asked for card he tells the player to "go fish" and the player must draw from the pile in the center. If the player draws the card he asked for, he may ask another player for a card. When a book is completed, it is placed face down in front of the player. If the player does not draw what he has asked for, then it is the next player's turn. The winner is the player with the most books when all books have been assembled.

Variation in Procedure:

A variation of this game is to have pairs of cards, for example *sands-sand, shoe-shoes,* and to have players "fish" for pairs instead of books.

Endings

Purpose: To provide practice in structural analysis

Materials: A number of cards with suffixes or word endings printed on them

Procedure:

Divide the class into two equal teams. On the chalkboard, list a number of familiar root words such as *run, sleep, help, rain, ask,* and *splash.* In a circle on the floor place flash cards lettered: *a, ed, d, ing,* and *y.* In the center of the circle a blindfolded team member is turned around. He points to a card and the blindfold is removed. He goes to the chalkboard, chooses a word and adds the ending to it (writing the new words on the board). He then pronounces the word. If the word is written correctly, he scores a point. If the word is pronounced correctly, he scores another point. If the word is written incorrectly, the rival team scores a point. The first team to receive twenty-five points wins.

16. Unable to Use Context Clues

RECOGNIZED BY

Pupil is unable to derive meaning and/or pronunciation of a word from the way it is used in a sentence.

DISCUSSION

The use of context clues can be one of the student's greatest helps in determining the meaning of unfamiliar words. It is often one of the easiest taught of the reading skills and yet many students are unaware that it can be an effective method of deriving the meaning and/or the pronunciation of words.

You can determine whether a student is having difficulties using context clues by listening to him read orally. While he reads, note whether words missed are ones that normally can be recognized from context. Also question the student about the meaning of certain words where that meaning is evident from the context. In silent reading ask the student to underline the words that he either does not know how to pronounce or define. The same procedure can be used in either case.

Do not expect a student to derive meaning from the context of the material if the material is too difficult. Material which falls into either the free or instructional reading levels probably will not be too difficult. On the other hand, material at a pupil's frustration level is too difficult to effectively make use of context clues. An explanation of these three levels is found in the section entitled "Definition of Terms."

RECOMMENDATIONS

A. Show the student that it is possible to derive the meaning of words from their context. Show specific examples.

1. The careless boy did his work in a *haphazard* manner.

2. He felt that although his work was *imperfect*, it was still good.

3. When he tried to *insert* the letter in the mailbox, the mailbox was too full.

4. They called in a *mediator* to help settle the problems between labor and management.

B. Use multiple choice questions in which the student fills in blanks: e.g., "Jack ____ a black pony (rock, rode, rod)." Using words which look alike also will give the student practice in phonic and strucural analysis.

C. Make tape recordings in which key words are omitted. Give the pupil a copy of the script and have him fill in the blank spaces as the tape is played.

D. Have the student practice reading up to a word, sounding at least the first sound, and then reading several words following the unknown word: "A cow and her c____ drank from the water hole (calf)." In this case the pupil should be able to say *calf* if it is in his listening-speaking vocabulary. He should also realize that a calf is the offspring of a cow.

E. Make sentences which can be completed by circling or underlining a picture, such as in the example.

Directions: Circle the picture that correctly completes the sentence.

The hen sat on her

F. Give a series of sentences in which only part of a word missing from context is spelled. See the examples.

1. The _ _ _ f _ ce of the water was smooth.

2. All of the Boy _ _ _ _ ts were cold when they arrived home.

3. The explorers climbed the _ _ _ nt _ _ n.

4. Is your son in the ar _ _ , _ _ vy, or m _ ri _ _ s?

G. Use pictures to illustrate certain words omitted from a tape-recorded story. Lay the pictures (approximately ten) in front of the pupil. As the recording is played, have the pupil pick up the picture that is appropriate to illustrate the missing words. Sound a bell for the missing word.

H. Make a series of sentences using words which are spelled alike but may have different pronunciations or meanings: *read, lead*. Have the pupil read sentences using these in proper context.

> She *read* the book.
> She will *read* the story.
> It was made out of *lead*.
> She had the *lead* in the play.

I.   Use commercially prepared materials designed especially for improving the student's ability to use context clues. (See Appendix B.)

17. Contractions Not Known

RECOGNIZED BY

Pupil is unable to pronounce contractions when he encounters them in print. For writing purposes, it is also important to be able to tell what two words each contraction stands for and/or to be able to make contractions from various words.

DISCUSSION

Because of my work with children and teachers during the past several years it has become apparent to me that a major problem experienced by students is their lack of knowledge of contractions. For example, many students whose reading simply "sounds poor" will be found to not know various contractions when their oral reading is coded and their specific problem is analyzed.

When testing for student's knowledge of contractions, the student should be shown the contraction and asked to pronounce it. If he can pronounce the word, it will usually suffice for reading purposes. (For example, for reading purposes he must read *can't,* but he does not necessarily know it means *cannot.*) You may wish to have the student tell what two words the contraction stands for so that you know whether he will be able to use it in his written work. Following is a list of contractions and the point at which they should be known.*

When Contractions Should Be Known

Age	Words		
2.9	can't	isn't	that's
	didn't	it's	wasn't
	hadn't	let's	won't
3.5	aren't	he's	there's
	don't	I'll	we'll
	hasn't	I'm	we're
	haven't	I've	what's
	he'll	she'll	wouldn't
	here's	she's	you're

---

* Ekwall, Eldon E. *Corrective Reading System* (Glenview, Illinois: Psychotechnics, Inc., 1976).

| **3.9** | ain't | they'd | |
| | couldn't | they're | |

4.5	anybody'd	they'll	who'd
	doesn't	they've	who'll
	he'd	we'd	you'd
	I'd	weren't	you'll
	she'd	we've	you've
	there'll	where's	

NOTE: 2.9 means the word should be known at the ninth month of the second grade, 3.5 means it should be known by the fifth month of the third grade, and so on. This information is based on an analysis of when these contractions were commonly taught in five sets of well-known basal readers.

In testing contractions you can type a stimulus sheet simply listing the contractions; however, leave off the level at which they should be known. Ask the student to read each contraction and then tell you what two words it stands for. Make an answer sheet such as in the example.

Name _____   School _____
Date _____   Testor _____

1. can't _____ _____

2. didn't _____ _____

If the student is able to tell you the contraction, place a plus (+) in the first blank. If he cannot, then place a zero (0) in the first blank. If he can tell you what two words it stands for, then place a plus (+) in the second blank—or a zero (0) in the second blank if he cannot.

RECOMMENDATIONS

A. For any contraction not known write the two words it stands for and then the contraction on the chalkboard. Have students make up sentences using both the contracted and noncontracted form. See the example.

let us   let's

1. Let us go with Mother and Father.

2. Let's go with Mother and Father.

B. Give matching exercises by placing a few contractions on slips in an envelope. Number each contraction. In the same envelope place the two words that each contraction stands for and place the matching number of the contraction on the back. Students should then try to match all contractions with their matching words by placing them side by side as appears in the example.

1. let's	let us
2. don't	do not

After the student has completed the exercise he can turn the cards in the right-hand column over to see if the numbers on the back match the numbers on the slips in the left-hand column.

C.   Give students paragraphs to read in which several words could be contracted. Underline these words. Instruct students to change words to a contraction as they read. See the example following.

Frank said to Jim, "We have only two days before you are going to leave." "Yes," said Jim, "I am waiting to go and I have already packed my suitcase."

After doing this type of exercise discuss why contractions are used and which form, long or short, sounds the most natural in common speech.

D.   Conduct contraction races between two students. Tell the students two words and see who can call out the contraction first. Also give contractions and have students call out the words they stand for.

E.   Give students newspaper articles and have them underline all contractions and words that could have been contracted.

F.   As children talk, call attention to the contractions they use by writing them down. Discuss why they used the contracted form.

18.   Fails to Comprehend

RECOGNIZED BY

Pupil cannot understand what he has read when questioned about the subject matter, or when simply asked to tell what he has read.

DISCUSSION

In order to comprehend well, a student must have acquired a vocabulary sufficient to cope with the material being read. He must also comprehend these words when they are then placed together in phrases, sentences and paragraphs. If the student must stop to puzzle over new words, he cannot be expected to comprehend well. Thus a prerequisite to adequate comprehension is a thorough knowledge of both the pronunciation and meaning of words. Attempting to teach comprehension once the student has learned his basic word attack skills will often be your most difficult problem. Perhaps the methods of teaching have contributed to the problem itself. Comprehension is tested but seldom *taught*. In fact, the only instruction some pupils receive in comprehension abilities is in the form of questions over a paragraph or story. This questioning may help; however, it evidently does so simply because we force students to learn to comprehend on their own.

Studies on the nature of comprehension have shown that although we often refer to comprehension subskills we cannot really prove these exist. About all we definitely know is that comprehension involves a word or vocabulary factor and then another group of skills which are difficult to prove exist as separate entities. We might simply refer to these as "other comprehension skills." Even though we cannot prove that these other comprehension skills exist it is perhaps useful to list some that we believe are useful for teaching purposes. These skills include the ability to:

1.   Recognize main ideas

2.   Recognize important details

3.   Develop visual images

4.   Predict outcomes

5.   Follow directions

6. Recognize the author's organization

7. Do critical reading

To decide whether or not a student is having problems with comprehension you might check the student's scores on the comprehension and vocabulary sections of standardized reading tests to determine whether the student is comprehending below his grade level. Have him read a 100–200-word passage from a basal reader at his grade level and ask questions testing his ability to remember facts, to make inferences, and to understand specific vocabulary words in order to determine the problem. Students who are having difficulties in comprehension will score less than 75 percent on reading material at their grade level. Use several reading passages and questions to insure a correct diagnosis. Finally, you may ask questions over material read concerning the specific abilities listed previously.

RECOMMENDATIONS

Vocabulary Development

Before a student can be expected to comprehend adequately he must develop a vocabulary sufficient to deal with words on the level on which he is expected to read.

A. Whenever new words come up in lessons, stop and discuss them in sufficient detail so that all students develop a concept of their meaning.

B. Appoint a "vocabulary committee" to preview each new lesson prior to class reading to select all words for which they do not know the meaning. Use these words as a guide to the new vocabulary along with the new vocabulary given in the textbook.

C. Develop pictures files for each unit in the students' textbook. Use the pictures to develop the meaning of new words and concepts. These pictures may be placed on a bulletin board or simply shown and discussed as each new unit is introduced.

D. Place pictures on the bulletin board and have students try to find as many words as possible to describe the pictures. If students are old enough to use a thesaurus, then allow them to do so. Place the words under the picture and discuss them every so often.

E. Develop "word awareness" by showing students how often we tend to skip over words for which we do not know the meaning. Promote awareness of new words by getting students to look for new words that they or other students may not know the meaning of. Write the new word on the chalkboard along with the name of the student who found it.

Carlos's new word—*idealism*

Frank's new word—*afterthought*

Discuss these words daily until most students know them. Keep adding new words to the bottom of the list and gradually erase the ones from the top after they have been discussed several times.

F.   Encourage students to use "vocabulary cards." As students read assignments or any other reading material have them search for new words. When a new word is found have them write it on a vocabulary card. Then have them write it in the sentence in which it was used and underline the word. Encourage use of meaning context. After they complete their reading, have them look the new word up in the dictionary and write its meaning. Then file the new vocabulary cards in a shoe box and review them periodically.

Ability to Recognize Main Ideas and Important Details

A. You should work with the pupil to help him find the main idea and important details of a story. You may list the main idea as well as the important details as shown in the following paragraph.

A little bird sang a song day after day. The old man had heard it so many times that he knew the tune by heart. Even the children who played nearby could sing it.

MAIN IDEA: A little bird sang his song day after day, after day.

SUPPORTING DETAILS: The old man had heard it many times.
The old man knew it by heart.
Even the children who played nearby could sing it.

Another way of bringing out the main idea of a paragraph and of showing the supporting details is to draw the paragraph as a diagram.

```
┌────────────────────────────────────────────────────┐
│  A little bird sang his song day after day, after day. │
└──┬─────────────────────────────────────────────────┘
   │  ┌──────────────────────────────────────────────┐
   │  │  The old man had heard it many times.         │
   │  ├──────────────────────────────────────────────┤
   │  │  The old man knew it by heart.                │
   │  ├──────────────────────────────────────────────┤
   │  │  Even the children who played nearby          │
   │  │  could sing it.                               │
   │  └──────────────────────────────────────────────┘
```

Other paragraphs may have two main ideas.

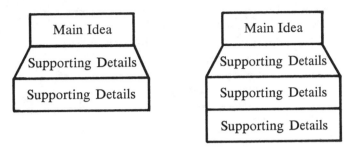

Other types of paragraphs may look like the following:

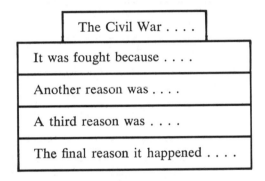

> But on the other hand there are the people who . . . .
>> Even some of these do not . . . .
>> Some do not even . . . .
>> Sometimes there are those who . . . .

> I will run for public office again if . . . .
>> Senator Brown must . . . .
>> Governor Turner should . . . .
>> My health . . . .
>> If I run I am sure . . . .

> The first reader introduces . . . .
> The second reader introduces . . . .
> The third reader discusses . . . .
> All of the readers in the series are deeply concerned with . . . .

> Once upon a time . . . .
> Therefore children, you should . . . .

When drawing paragraphs with the children do not expect to find complete agreement on how they should look. Keep in mind that the important thing is to get the students thinking about paragraph structure. When using this system you may want to have the students suggest names for certain common structure patterns; for example, the logical conclusion, the sales pitch, and the conditional. However do not try this technique in the early stages of pattern development as the students will try to fit new structures into old forms.

B. Read the introduction or title to the story or a chapter and then anticipate with the children what the author is going to say.

C. Select appropriate titles for paragraphs, chapters, or short selections. You might also have the children select the best title from several listed.

D. After reading a paragraph have the children tell in their own words what the author has said.

E. Many books have subheadings in dark print. Turn these subheadings into questions and then read specifically to answer those questions.

F. Use a series of three pictures, one of which represents the main idea of a paragraph. Have the pupil pick the one that best represents the main idea of the paragraph or have the students make these and put them on cards, i.e., one paragraph and three pictures on a card.

G. Have the pupils underline the sentences in paragraphs that best represent the main idea. Make sure there *is* a best sentence, and also make sure the paragraph has a main idea.

Ability to Recognize Important Details

A. Discuss with the children the important details in several paragraphs. Children often focus on minor dates and details which are not really important. Perhaps the testing often used encourages this type of reading.

B. Help the child to find the main idea, then ask him to find significant details which describe or elaborate upon the idea.

C. Ask the children to write down all the details from a selection. Have them classify the details from their list as (1) important, (2) helpful, but not essential, and (3) unnecessary.

D. Have the children answer questions or complete sentences that require a knowledge of the important details.

E. Have the children draw a series of pictures to illustrate the details; for example, the description of a scene.

Ability to Develop Visual Images

A. For children to visualize a certain setting or image effectively they must have actually or vicariously experienced it. Review the setting of a story with children before they begin. You could also supplement their information with a film or filmstrip or have children bring pictures from books and magazines.

B.   As a child reads a selection, you might stop him from time to time and ask him to describe images gained from the reading. Also he might be asked questions combining the images from the passage and his own imaginings. For example: "What color coat do you think the person is wearing?" "Was it a big tiger or a little tiger?"

C.   Discuss figures of speech such as *big as a bear, black as pitch* or *as cold as a polar bear in the Yukon.* Help the children to see that figurative language can really add meaning to a story or in some cases may be misleading. Ask the children to listen for and collect various figures of speech.

D.   Ask the children to draw pictures of certain settings they have read about. Compare and discuss.

Ability to Predict Outcomes

A.   Show a series of pictures from a story and ask the children to tell, either in writing or orally, what they think the story will be about.

B.   Read to a certain point in a story and then ask the children to tell or write their versions of the ending.

C.   Ask the children to read the chapter headings of a book and predict what the story will be about. Read the story and compare versions.

D.   Encourage the children to be accurate in their predictions and to be ready to revise their preconceived ideas in the light of new information.

Ability to Follow Directions

A.   Write directions for paper folding, etc., which the students can do at their seats. Have the children read and perform these directions step by step.

B.   Write directions for recess activities on the chalkboard. Try to get the students in the habit of following these directions without oral explanation.

C.   Ask the children to write directions for playing a game. Have them read their directions and analyze whether they could learn to play the game from a certain child's written directions.

D.   Encourage the children to read written directions such as those in workbooks and certain arithmetic problems without your help.

E.   Use commercially prepared material designed for improving ability to follow directions. (See Appendix B.)

Ability to Recognize the Author's Organization

A.   Discuss the fact that all authors have some form of organization in mind when writing. Look over chapter headings and discuss other possibilities for organization. Do the same with shorter selections as well as paragraphs by themselves.

B.   Discuss the author's use of pictures, graphs, charts, and diagrams to clarify certain concepts.

C.   Discuss the use of introductory material, dark headings, study questions, and summaries.

D.   Explain the value of "signal" words and phrases in showing organizational patterns.

E.   Make the children aware of "signal words" and "signal phrases" in selections: *to begin with, next, not long after, then, finally, several factors were responsible for, these led to, which further complicated it by.*

F.   Write down a sequence of events from a story the children have read and ask them to number the events in the order in which they happened. Explain before they read the story what they will be expected to do.

G.   Write each of the sentences from a paragraph on a separate (small) piece of paper. Ask the pupils to arrange these sentences in a logical chain of events in order to form a paragraph that makes sense.

H.   Cut up comic strips or pictures of sequential events and have the children assemble them in their correct order.

Ability to do Critical Reading
A higher level reading skill

A.   Analyze editorials for the author's purpose.

B.   Tape-record advertisements heard on the radio and TV and discuss the merit of certain statements.

C.   Analyze speeches given by and articles written by politicians.

D.   Analyze stories and poems for morals they may teach or for other motives the author may have had.

GAMES AND EXERCISES FOR VOCABULARY DEVELOPMENT

Matching Words and Definitions

Purpose: To enrich vocabulary

Materials: Envelopes containing slips of paper with words printed on them. The envelopes should also contain a larger second set of slips with a definition for each word.

Procedure:

Have students each take an envelope and empty it out on their desks. They should then place the word slips in a column in numerical order.

1. candid

2. slipshod

They then try to match the definition slips with the words. The definition slips should have a number that corresponds with the word slip; however, the number should appear only on the back. This way students can check on the accuracy of their work when they have finished. Number each envelope and give students a number sheet corresponding to each envelope. Have them check off each number as they do the words in each envelope. This way each student will be sure to do each envelope.

Homonym Concentration

Purpose: To enlarge vocabulary

Materials: Sets of cards (about eight to ten) with an equal number of homonyms on them (total of sixteen to twenty)

Procedure:

Play the game the same as "Concentration." Shuffle the cards and place them facedown in rows on a table or on a concentration board with squares on it. Two students play. One begins by turning over a card and then trying to turn over another card with a homonym of the first card. If he fails, he turns both cards facedown and the next student takes his turn. Whenever a student turns over a pair of homonyms he gets to keep the cards. The student with the most cards at the end of the game is the winner. (This same exercise may be done with antonyms and synonyms.)

Phrase It Another Way

Purpose: To enrich vocabulary

Materials: Phrase cards or phrases written on the chalkboard

Procedure:

Each day a new phrase is placed on the chalkboard that is commonly used by students or you in daily conversation and activities. Opposite the phrase is another way of saying the commonly used phrase. Each day you and the students concentrate on using the phrase in a new way. You may wish to place the phrases on chart paper and display them as the number grows.

Old phrase	*Phrasing it another way*
My work is done	My work is completed
He runs fast	He is a rapid runner
He couldn't get it	He was deprived of it

Drawing New Words

Purpose: To build vocabulary and improve dictionary skills

Materials: A number of 3" x 5" cards with new vocabulary words written in a sentence (underline the new word)
Dictionary

Procedure:

The cards are shuffled and placed facedown on the table. Students then take turns picking up a card, reading the sentence, and defining the underlined word. Another student looks up the word in the dictionary to see if the definition was correct.

New Word for the Day

Purpose: To enrich vocabulary

Materials: Word cards for new and old words

Procedure:

Decide on a new word that can be substituted for one that is commonly used each day (see example). Place the old and new word in a chart holder. During the day attempt to use the new word whenever it comes up instead of using the old word. This should be done by you as well as by students. Discuss how doing this type of activity will enlarge vocabularies and make students' talk sound more "mature."

Old word(s)	*New word*
talk	discuss
hate	dislike
do better	improve

GAMES AND EXERCISES FOR OTHER COMPREHENSION SKILLS

Story Division

Purpose: To provide practice in comprehension and oral reading skills for pupils who lack self-confidence

Materials: A basal reader of which each pupil has a copy

Procedure:

You first divide a story such as the following into parts:

1. Toddle was Pam's pet turtle.
   He liked to crawl.
   He got out of his pan of water and crawled all around the house.

2. Toddle bumped into things.
   Bang! Bang! Down they went.
   Mother did not like this.

3. She said, "Please, Pam, put Toddle back into the water, and do make him stay there."

Each child studies *one* part of the story and reads it orally. After a whole story is read, the children are given a comprehension check.

This type of procedure gives the children confidence because they know which part they will be required to read, and they can practice reading it silently before reading it orally.

A Matching Board

Purpose: To provide practice on the various components of comprehension

Materials: A piece of ½" plywood the same size as a sheet of ditto paper
             Shoestrings

Procedure:

Drill holes (1½" apart) down the center of the piece of plywood as shown following. Make holes down the entire length of the board, spacing them the same vertical distance as four spaces on a typewriter. The holes should be just large enough to let the shoestrings pass through them quite easily. Attach shoestrings through the holes in the left column. Tie a knot on the back side so that they will not pull out frontwards. Make sure that each string in the left column is long enough to thread through any hole in the right column.

Ditto various exercises such as sentence completion, missing words from the context of a sentence, word opposites, sentence opposites, etc. Make each set of opposites four vertical typewriter lines spaces so that they will correspond with the holes on the board. Use a thumbtack or transparent tape at the top and bottom of each column of questions and answers to hold the dittoed material in place. Use these boards with individual children to provide practice in areas in which they need special help. Various kinds of exercises are illustrated following.

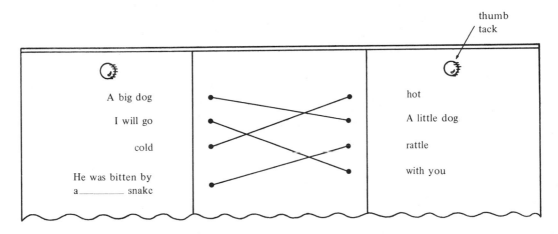

Main Ideas

Purpose: To improve the students' ability to concentrate and to locate the main idea in a selection

Materials: Basal readers, science or social studies textbooks

Procedure:

Before giving the children a reading assignment, show them a list of true-false questions concerning the material on the reading assignment. Construct the questions so that they test for the main ideas of paragraphs from the reading material. This test will give the students an idea of what they are expected to gather from the assignment and it will improve their ability to recognize main ideas in future reading. Make sure that students understand that the questions test for main ideas and not for details.

Directions: Some of the statements below are true and some are false. Write *T* after the true statements and *F* after those that are not true.

1. Carlos did not really want to race his car. ＿＿＿＿＿

2. The weather was just right for racing. ＿＿＿＿＿

3. Someone had been fooling around with Carlos's car. ＿＿＿＿＿

4. Most of Carlos's friends felt that he could win the race
    if he wanted to. _____

Picture Puzzle

Purpose: To help children recognize, evaluate, and describe various situations

Materials: Pictures clipped from magazines or old discarded readers mounted on
            tagboard
            Word cards
            Flannel board

Procedure:

Display a picture on a flannel board. Allow the children to select from a large
number of word cards the ones they feel best describe the given picture. Place
these word cards on the flannel board with the picture and discuss their appropri-
ateness to the situation.

Variation in Procedure:

Use the same procedure as above except substitute sentence strips for the individual word cards or make sentences from the individual cards.

Riddles

Purpose: To provide practice in the comprehension of descriptive details

Materials: Tagboard

Procedure:

Write a series of short stories describing a particular object or animal. Have the
children read the story and decide what the object or animal is. In the bottom cor-
ner, under a flap of paper, place the correct answer. The children may check their
answers after they have made their decision. See the example.

My home is in the country.
I live on a farm.
The farmer's children take care of me.
They give me grain and water.
I give them eggs.
I am a good friend of yours.
What animal am I?

Answer
is here

What Do You See?

Purpose: To develop picture-word description relationships

Materials: Pictures cut from magazines
Tagboard
Flannel board

Procedure:

Place pictures of objects on a flannel board. On tagboard write some questions concerning the pictures and some questions which will act as distractors. Have the children answer the questions in relation to the pictures posted.

Do you see a frog?

Do you see a hopping rabbit?

Do you see a fat pig?

Do you see a door?

Do you see an open window?

Do you see a red ball?

The Wizard

Purpose: To provide practice in reading for specific questions

Materials: A basal reader of which each child has a copy

Procedure:

One pupil is chosen as The Wizard. He asks a question relating to the reading lesson and calls on a classmate to answer. If that child answers correctly, he is The Wizard and he makes up the next question. Those children who do not answer a question correctly have another chance to be The Wizard with further play.

Classification Game

Purpose: To develop the ability to classify related words

Materials: Pocket chart
                Word cards
                Envelopes

Procedure:

Divide the pocket chart into four columns. In the first three columns in each row place three related word cards. Leave the fourth column blank and have the children select a word card from their envelopes that belongs in the same class as the other three words in that row.

car	boat	airplane	_____
ball	top	doll	_____
Susan	Bill	Lassie	_____
walk	gallop	skip	_____
red	blue	green	_____

Variation in Procedure:

Instead of filling in the missing word as described above, use four words in which one word does not fit the category represented by the other three words. Have children find and remove the "misfit."

As I See It

Purpose: To provide children with an opportunity to express the visual images they gain from reading or hearing a story

Materials: A story (preferably one with vividly described scenes)
                Drawing paper and paints or colors

Procedure:

After the children have heard or read a story have them illustrate various scenes as they perceived them. After drawing the scenes, mix them up in a box and have one child stand in front of the room and pull out pictures. After he has chosen a picture, he will try to reconstruct the story on a bulletin board from the many pictures that are in the box. Discuss various differences in drawings and discuss why some pupils interpreted certain things differently from others. At times you will want to re-read certain parts of the story to see if material was interpreted incorrectly.

Furnish the Empty Room

Purpose: To develop the ability to recognize appropriate visual images

Materials: Flannel board
            Pictures of specific objects cut from magazines or old books

Procedure:

At the top of the flannel board place printed subject headings such as *kitchen* or *playroom*. Have the children select object pictures that are appropriate to the given headings.

My Image

Purpose: To encourage the building of sensory images

Materials: Various materials to create sounds which are very familiar, somewhat familiar, and less familiar to children

Procedure:

Have the children close their eyes and listen as you or another child makes a noise. Have the children open their eyes and write words or phrases that describe the noise. Then have them draw pictures which represent the noise. Encourage them to use a varied vocabulary in their descriptions.

That Makes Sense

Purpose: To develop the ability to associate objects with their sources and to develop the ability to logically complete a given idea

Materials: Pocket chart
              Word cards
              Envelopes

Procedure:

A series of incomplete statements are placed on the pocket chart. Word cards containing the appropriate missing words or phrases are provided for the children. From these they will select the correct answer and place it in the pocket chart next to the incomplete idea.

A dress is made from	in the ground
Fish usually	flour
Cocoa is made from	fly
Oil can come from	seeds
Cabbage grows	beans
Parrots can	on the ground
Strawberries have	swim in water
Cakes are made from	whales
Potatoes grow	wool

Ordered Phrases

Purpose: To provide practice in skimming and in determining sequence (comprehension)

Materials: Cards with phrases copied from a story, book, or basal reader

Procedure:

Have the children read the book and place the phrases on the cards in columns in the order that the phrases occurred on the page.

You should also write the number order on the back of the cards. Such numbering will enable a child to correct his own work.

Sentence Puzzles

Purpose: To help children see a sequence of ideas

Materials: Envelopes
Paragraphs or short stories that are written in a somewhat logical order

Procedure:

Cut up the stories and/or paragraphs into sentences and paste each sentence on a small rectangular piece of paper. Place one story or paragraph in each envelope. Pass these envelopes out to the children and have them assemble the stories in a logical order. Number the envelopes and have the children keep a record of the stories or paragraphs (by envelope number) that they have assembled. The children continue to exchange these envelopes until all have had a turn at each envelope. In some cases you may want to have stories or paragraphs graded according to the reading level of a particular group. In such a case Reading Group B will do only those envelopes marked *1-B, 2-B,* and so forth.

It Does—It Doesn't

Purpose: To help children classify words according to descriptive specifications

Materials: Pocket chart
Envelopes
Word cards

Procedure:

Divide the pocket chart into two columns. Place a statement and its opposite next to one another at the top of the chart. Provide each child with an envelope of word cards containing current vocabulary words. Have the children classify the words found in their envelopes according to the given statements. Use a great variety of statements and words cards which will require careful thought. Vocabulary and classification sentences will vary with grade levels.

It can walk	It cannot walk

Word Cards

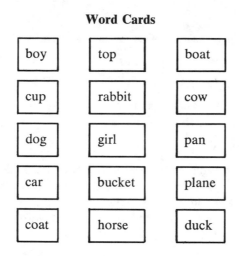

boy	top	boat
cup	rabbit	cow
dog	girl	pan
car	bucket	plane
coat	horse	duck

What Did It Say?

Purpose: To develop phrase recognition and the ability to follow directions

Materials: Flash cards

Procedure:

Write specific directions on individual flash cards. As the cards are flashed before the class, call on certain students to see who can respond. For example:

1. Close the door.
2. Give a pencil to a brown-eyed boy.
3. Stand up. Turn three circles. Touch the desk behind yours.
4. Draw a circle inside of a triangle on the board.

Story Pantomime

Purpose: To provide practice in reading for information and following directions

Materials: Cards on which are printed directions for acting out a certain activity

Procedure:

The cards are passed out to all the pupils in the class. One pupil is selected to act out each set. The other pupils watch critically for the complete acting of every detail in the directions.

Example: Pretend you are washing dishes. Stop up the sink, open the doors under the sink, and get the soap. Put the soap in the sink, turn the faucet on, test the water, put the dishes in the water, and then wash and rinse three dishes. Put the dishes in the dish rack to dry.

A story pantomime might also include such things as the following:

> drawing water from a well
> making the bed
> rocking the baby
> picking flowers for a bouquet
> singing a hymn
> winding the clock
> watering the flowers
> ironing
> picking and eating apples
> playing baseball

Good Words-Bad Words

Purpose: To provide practice in critical reading, especially concerning the purpose the author had in mind when the material was written

Materials: Various written or tape-recorded advertisements

Procedure:

Have the children locate and circle or make a list of words that they can classify as either "good" words or "bad" words. Good words might include such words as *freedom, well-being, Number One rating,* and *delicious.* Bad words might include words such as *disease, cracks, peels,* and *odor.* Discuss how the use of these words influence our thinking about a certain product. Carry this exercise into the study of certain characters in books of whom the author wishes to convey a good or bad impression.

19. Unaided Recall Scanty

RECOGNIZED BY

Pupil is unable to remember what he has read when asked to recall what was in a passage.

DISCUSSION

Pupils sometimes are able to fill in blanks by using a word that was used in context in a passage they have read. They also may be able to recall other events if they are given a hint of some kind as to what a certain passage contained. Some students, however, cannot remember what they have read when they are simply asked, "What did you read?" This is, of course, the type of situation the student will find himself in many times in later life. A student's failure to recall what was read may be caused by a lack of comprehension. In this case the suggestions for improving comprehension (see Section 18, p. 88) may be helpful. A student also may be hampered in his ability to recall what he has read because the vocabulary is too difficult for him. He should be able to pronounce at least 95 percent of the words correctly. If he cannot do so, he cannot be expected to adequately recall and comprehend what he reads.

RECOMMENDATIONS

A. Use easier material in which the student is able to pronounce 95 percent or more of the words correctly.

B. Discuss the material, review the vocabulary, and use illustrations where possible to build up a background of information on the subject before the students attempt to read it.

C. Use reading material which appeals to the reader and which portrays vividly a chain of events.

D. Ask the students to visualize and then draw a scene described by a reading passage. Compare drawings and discuss pictures that were not complete because the student could not recall the descriptive features.

E. Have the students underline events as they occur in a reading passage. They may also number events that occur in succession.

F.   Discuss the story's setting thoroughly before reading it. This will help the students to draw parallels to their own experiences and thus remember better.

G.   Make the student aware of key words such as *in the beginning, after that, and then,* and *lastly,* that authors use to show a series of events. This awareness is especially useful in social studies.

20. Response Poorly Organized

RECOGNIZED BY

Pupil is unable to state or write events as they occurred in a passage he has read.

DISCUSSION

A student whose response is poorly organized probably does not comprehend well. For this reason you should first determine if a student cannot organize his thoughts well or if he does not understand what he has read. He cannot be expected to correctly organize material that is too difficult for him. You should be sure that practice materials are on the student's free or instructional level.

RECOMMENDATIONS

A. List the events that took place in a story. Have the students number them according to the order in which they took place. Have the students do the numbering in the reading material as they are reading it; test on the same material afterwards.

B. Show the students how "signal words" can give a clue to the order of a chain of events.

C. Cut paragraphs apart and have the students put them together in a logical sequences, such as in the following.

*Once upon a time there was a giant who lived in a very old castle.

zThe giant was tall and thin.

!He had lived in the castle for many years.

#He looked as though he had not had enough to eat.

Use a designation as *, z, !, # for each sentence. After the students complete their paragraphs, discuss the variations in structure: e.g., would it have been more logical to have had a sequence of *, !, z, # in this paragraph?

D. Ask the students to try to visualize the story and project themselves into it. Building up a background for the story before reading it will help the students to visualize events. This background of information may be simply a discussion of the events and the surroundings of the story, or it may be in the form of a film or filmstrip relating to the story.

E.   Have the students put a short story in outline form. Use this method sparingly.

F.   Give the students a partially completed outline of a story. Have them read the story and then complete the outline. See the following example:

The Giant of Red Marble Castle

The giant lived in a very old castle.

The first thing the giant did when he got up
in the morning was _____.
After that, he would usually _____.

One day when the giant was very hungry he decided to
___ _____.

First he got his _____.
Then he got a _____.

After he had killed the _____.
He _____ it first.
Then he _____.

21. Low Rate of Speed

RECOGNIZED BY

Pupil is unable to read as many words per minute as would be normal for a pupil of his age on a certain kind of reading material.

DISCUSSION

You can determine whether certain pupils are slow readers by giving a timed reading exercise to an entire class. The various reading speeds listed in words per minute can be graphed or charted to determine which students are considerably below average on a particular kind of material for their class. When giving timed exercises you should choose several pages which are normal reading material in story reading. You should not use pages containing questions, lists, etc. Timed exercises from two to five minutes should be sufficient. You seldom need to worry about achieving a very rapid reading rate in the elementary grades. Therefore, the suggestions listed under (A), (B), (C), and (D) are more appropriate for junior or senior high level students. The suggestions listed under (E) and (F) should be appropriate for any level above the primary grades.

RECOMMENDATIONS

A. Have the pupils pace their reading with their hands. They should attempt to move across the page slightly faster than their comfortable reading speed normally allows. It should, however, be emphasized that the hand paces the eyes and the reading speed and not the opposite.

B. Focus on speed by using material which can be read fast. Give timed reading exercises followed by comprehension questions. Let the student keep his own chart on speed and comprehension. See Appendix C for sample chart.

C. For the older students, assign or let them pick short paperback novels that are meant to be read rapidly. Use these in conjunction with hand pacing to practice for speed.

D. Use reading material which highly motivates the student. Let him choose the stories for practice.

E.   Explain to the pupils that in some types of reading it is important to be able to read at a high rate of speed.

GAMES AND EXERCISES

Timed Research

Purpose: To encourage rapid reading

Materials: Some 3″ x 5″ cards
Trade books

Procedure:

Keep a file of cards in a box. On each card put information such as the following:

1.   The name of the book is _____ .
2.   In the chapter that describes the finding of the treasure chest, answer the following questions:
3.   You should allow yourself eight minutes to read this chapter after you have found the page number.

During a regular reading period devoted to increasing reading speed the children will come up to your desk and take a card. They should then follow the instructions on the card. CAUTION! Do not require a lot of writing for the answers, but rather keep them very short. The purpose of the questions is only to allow you to check on comprehension.

The time limit you wish to set for reading a story will be determined by the grade level of the students involved and, of course, by the number of words or pages. This is also a good way to motivate the students to do further reading.

Timed Stories

Purpose: To encourage rapid reading while still focusing on improving comprehension

Materials: A number of envelopes with short stories on them along with sets of questions over each story

Procedure:

Prior to doing this, you should have given speed reading tests to your class and grouped them accordingly; i.e., one group which reads from 75–100 words per minute, one group which reads from 100–125 words per minute, etc. Cut a number of short stories from old basal readers. Put one of these stories along with approximately ten comprehension questions in an envelope. Develop norms for each story; for example, a certain story for the 100–125 group may be labeled as an eight-minute story. Label the envelopes under headings such as *Dog Stories, Family Life Stories,* and *Science Stories.* Let the students choose the stories they want to read. From the labeling the students will know that they should read the story in a certain number of minutes. This technique is a change from the timed test in which each student is reading the same subject matter. It also avoids having the faster readers waiting for the slower readers, because when they finish a story they can get an envelope and begin another story. Have the children keep a record of the stories they have read and their percent of comprehension on each story.

22. High Rate of Reading at the Expense of Accuracy

RECOGNIZED BY

Pupil finishes reading assignments before the rest of the class and consequently lacks comprehension of what he has read.

DISCUSSION

Reading at a high rate of speed is not always undesirable. There are, however, certain types of reading material which should be read more slowly than others. For example, mathematics and much of our science reading matter requires slow, more careful reading. Many students are not able to adjust their reading rate downward as the reading material becomes difficult. This situation is especially true of the student who constantly reads novels or the newspaper and is then required to read material which requires considerable concentration.

You may occasionally find a student in the lower elementary grades who reads at a rate that impairs his accuracy. The problem is more prevalent, however, with older students who have become accustomed to reading material which requires little concentration.

RECOMMENDATIONS

A.   Discuss the various reading speeds which are desirable for certain types of material. Show the students as well as tell them.

B.   From material found in a reading passage give oral and written questions which require accurate answers. Let the student know ahead of time that he will be required to answer questions over the reading passage.

C.   Give the students worksheets which contain reading passages along with questions about subject matter in the reading passages. Ask them to underline the answers to questions as they read them.

D.   Give the students study guide questions over material they are to read. Many books contain questions over a unit or chapter at the end of that unit or chapter. Encourage the students to read these questions before they begin reading the material in the chapter or unit.

23. Voicing-Lip Movement

RECOGNIZED BY

Pupil reads with visible lip movement and/or voicing of words.

DISCUSSION

A pupil who continually voices words as he reads silently is not likely to gain any real speed until he can be taught that it is not necessary to "pronounce" each word he reads. Many people unconsciously pronounce words to themselves even though they do not actually move their lips in doing so. Much voicing and lip movement can be detected by simply watching for visible signs which are apparent when someone speaks. Other students may voice words and yet show no visible signs of doing so. One way to determine whether a student is voicing words is to simply ask him. Very slow, silent reading is also a sign that a pupil may be voicing words. That in itself, however, is not enough evidence to support such a diagnosis. Remember that voicing or lip movement is often an indication that a student is reading in material which is too difficult for him. By giving him material that is considerably easier and then noting whether the voicing and lip movement continues or stops, you can determine whether the cause is habit or simply an indication that the student has been reading at or near his frustration level.

RECOMMENDATIONS

A.   As the student reads, have him hold his mouth shut with his teeth firmly together. Tell him to hold his tongue against the roof of his mouth.

B.   Have the students pace their reading with their hands. Make sure the rate they use is faster than they normally speak. Do not attempt to do this with children in first, second, or third grade.

C.   Use controlled reading devices which require reading at a rate too fast for voicing words. (See Appendix B.) Do not attempt to do this with children in first, second, or third grade.

24. Inability to Skim

RECOGNIZED BY

Pupil is unable to rapidly spot certain phrases, facts, or words as he skims or scans reading material.

DISCUSSION

One of the causes of the inability to skim is that the students have not felt a need for this skill. People who actually need to learn to skim and who are shown how to do so, soon become adept at this skill. Teachers who are attempting to improve the ability to skim need to show students how to skim as well as merely testing their ability to do so.

Those pupils who are not adept at skimming can usually be found by using the following procedure. List five to ten facts, dates, sentences, etc. which appear in a lesson and then give the students the assignment of finding the material after a reasonable time limit has been set. Watch for those who have only a little done when the faster ones have finished.

There has been no attempt to differentiate between the terms *skim* and *scan* in this book.

RECOMMENDATIONS

A. Hold a class discussion on how skimming can be beneficial to persons such as the student and the businessman. Try to determine when it is appropriate for the student to skim. A list of times when skimming may be appropriate might be similar to the following:

   1. looking for a name in a telephone book

   2. looking for a date in a history book

   3. looking for a certain number of factors to solve a problem

   4. reading the newspaper and searching for a certain article

    5.   wanting an idea of what an article or book will be about

    6.   looking for a word in a dictionary

B.   Show the pupils how to move their hands down a page in a telephone directory to find a certain name. After they have practiced and have become proficient with their hands, they can usually do as well without the use of their hands.

C.   Give the students copies of newspapers and have them skim over them to find things such as the article about the president, or a baseball pitcher. Another good exercise with a newspaper is to have the students find a phrase on a certain page which describes something or tells a certain fact. After the students have found the phrase, ask them to paraphrase the author.

D.   Give study questions on a reading assignment which can be answered by skimming the material. Keep in mind that this is not always the type of reading one wants to encourage.

E.   Have the students skim to find a certain word in the dictionary.

F.   Have the students skim to find a certain word (name of a city, etc.) or date in a history book.

G.   Tell what a certain paragraph is about and then have the pupils skim to find the topic sentence of that paragraph. (Make sure there is one!)

H.   Show the children that is possible to get the meaning of some material when many words are missing. Make paragraphs in which some words *unnecessary* for comprehension are missing. Make sure they understand that they are not to try to supply the missing words. Another variation of this exercise is to give the children paragraphs and have them underline only the words that are really necessary for comprehension. See the example.

> The *superintendent* of *schools* in *Huntsville* spoke to a large audience. She *discussed reasons* for the *new building program.* To *some extent, she covered methods* by which *new revenue* might be made *available.* Everyone thought her *speech was excellent.*

GAMES AND EXERCISES

Skim and Sort

Purpose: To provide practice in skimming

Materials: Old textbooks with stories in them that are somewhat varied
                Envelopes

Procedure:

Cut three stories from a book and then cut each story into either paragraphs or fairly short passages. Make sure each paragraph or passage contains some subject matter that gives a clue to which story it came from. Mix all of the paragraphs and/or passages together and place them in an envelope. Write the names of the three stories on the outside of the envelope. Give the children these envelopes and have them sort through them rapidly, putting each paragraph or passage in one of three piles to match the story title. Number each paragraph and/or passage. When a child has finished sorting these, give him the number key to check his work. (For example, numbers 1, 3, 5, 7, 9, 13, 15, and 16 may belong in the first story, numbers 2, 6, 8, 14, 17, and 18 may belong in the second story, and numbers 4, 10, 11, 12, 19, and 20 may belong in the third story.)

Finish It

Purpose: To provide practice in skimming

Materials: A book of which all children in the game have a copy

Procedure:

Give a page from which you are going to read. Every member of the class turns to that page. You then begin reading somewhere on that page. After reading a few words you stop and those who have found the place continue to read to the end of the sentence.

Skimming Race

Purpose: To provide practice in skimming

Materials: Any book which is available to every child in the game

Procedure:

Divide the children into two groups or let captains choose sides. Either you or alternating captains ask a question and then tell the children the page where the answer can be found. The first child to find the answer stands by his seat. The first person standing is called upon to read the answer. A correct answer scores one point for that side. The object is to see who can get the most points in a specified amount of time or in a specified number of questions. If a child stands and then gives a wrong answer take away one point from his side.

Rapid Search

Purpose: To provide children with practice in skimming

Materials: Several copies of the same articles in magazines, basal readers, or newspapers

Procedure:

One child finds a part of the story which represents some action. He then pantomimes this action and the rest of the children skim rapidly to try to find the sentence in the story which describes the actions of the child doing the pantomiming.

25. Inability to Adjust Reading Rate to the Difficulty of the Material

RECOGNIZED BY

The student reads at the same rate regardless of the *type* of material he is reading.

DISCUSSION

Many people are in the habit of reading all kinds of material at one speed. They read a newspaper or novel as though it were a science book or a set of directions. This is a habit that can be overcome easily if the student is shown how varying his reading rate can save him time and/or improve his comprehension.

To determine whether a student is reading all kinds of material at the same speed, simply give him a speed test on several kinds of material. The first material should be of the type found in novels or in a newspaper. Then give another speed test on material which would require more careful reading such as the expository writing in a science book. If the student reads all of the material at approximately the same rate, he is undoubtedly having problems adjusting his reading rate to the difficulty of the material.

RECOMMENDATIONS

A.   Discuss various types of reading material and show the students how rates should vary on these materials. You may wish to construct a chart to explain this idea.

How We Read Different Kinds of Materials

Skim

1. Telephone book
2. Newspaper (when looking for one thing)

Medium

1. Our history assignments

Fast

1. Novels
2. Normal reading of newspaper

Slow

1. Procedures for experiments in science
2. Our mathematics book
3. Explanations in our English books

B.   Time an entire class on a reading passage from a novel, and then time them on a reading passage from a mathematics book, preferably one which explains a process. Compare the average amount of time that was taken to read each passage or the number of words read in a certain amount of time. Emphasize that comprehension is necessary in both cases.

C.   Check the students' comprehension on easy and difficult material when each is read fast and when each is read slowly. Determine proper reading speeds for adequate comprehension of each type of material.

D.   Much of the material in science and social studies is set up with a number of dark headings within the chapters. The student should study this material in the following manner:

   1.   Turn the first dark heading into a question; for example, the heading may state: **The New World.** The student would then make a question of this by saying, "Where was the New World?"

   2.   Then he would read to answer that question.

   3.   When he has read down to the next dark heading he should stop and try to answer the question he had just posed. If he cannot answer it, then he should read the material again. If he can answer it, then he should proceed to the next dark heading and do the same with it.

E.   Discuss when it is not necessary to read every word, such as in a descriptive passage of scenery in a novel or details in newspaper articles. Have students underline only those parts that would be necessary for adequate comprehension. Then have students exchange articles or pages of a novel and read only the parts that other students have underlined. Discuss information derived by various students by reading only the underlined material. Ask the students who underlined the material to comment on the adequacy of the second reader's comprehension.

26. *Written Recall Limited to Spelling Ability*

RECOGNIZED BY

Student is unable to spell enough words correctly to express his answers on paper.

DISCUSSION

Discovering that a pupil makes a great number of mistakes in spelling presents no difficulty for the teacher. However, there is a reasonably high correlation between reading and spelling ability. The types of errors made in one may indicate that the same types of errors are present in the other. The pupil who is a phonetic speller may tend to mispronounce words which are phonetically irregular. Similarly, the pupil who uses almost no phonetic word attack may lack the ability to spell for the same reason. By carefully observing the way a student reads and spells you may note certain problem areas which will be helpful in determining specific kinds of suggestions for help.

A student who is not able to learn as many words as would be normal for his age/grade level should be taught a mastery list or the most commonly used words. If he must cut down on the total number of words learned, then the words sacrificed should be those of less utility. Be sure that in *all* subject matter you emphasize spelling. This strategy will help in motivating the children to improve their spelling and will give them the feeling that it is important to spell correctly all the time and not just during the spelling period. Try to determine the mode of learning in which each child is most successful (visual, oral, aural, aural-oral, kinesthetic) and place him in a group to be taught in that particular manner. Furthermore, teach spelling rules inductively and provide for use of newly learned words.

RECOMMENDATIONS

A. Pronounce the word clearly, then have the child pronounce it. Use the word in a sentence and have the child use it in a sentence. Write the word on the chalkboard, or, when working with a single child, write it on a piece of paper. Have the child write the word on a card (8½″ x 3″). Underline syllables and discuss letter combinations. When underlining syllables it may be more effective to use different colors for different syllables. The child can use the card for further study. These cards should be kept in a file such as in an old shoe box.

B.   In working with children whose spelling is too phonetic (e.g., *nees* for *knees,* or *wun* for *one*) you should concentrate on showing the child the "whole word picture" rather than focusing on sounds within words.

C.   Never let the child spell the word wrong in the beginning.

D.   Keep increasing the spelling vocabulary by adding previously missed words to new lists as well as some words with which students are more familiar. Most children can learn more words than normally would be assigned to them in a spelling book.

E.   Teach the following spelling rules by guiding the children to discover them for themselves:

   1.   Write *ie* when the sound is *ee,* except after *c,* or when sounded like *a* as in *neighbor* and *weight,* or *i* as in *height.*

   2.   When the prefixes *il, im, in, un, dis, mis,* and *over* are added to a word, the spelling of the original word remains the same.

   3.   When the suffixes *ness* and *ly* are added to a word, the spelling of the word remains the same. Examples: *mean + ness = meanness; final + ly = finally.*

   4.   With words ending in *y,* change the *y* to *i* before adding the suffix. Examples: *read + ily = readily; heavy + ness = heaviness.*

   5.   Drop the final *e* before a suffix beginning with a vowel. Examples: *care + ing = caring, write + ing = writing.* (Exceptions: *noticeable, courageous, dyeing. Dyeing* is spelled as such to prevent confusion with *dying.*)

   6.   Keep the final *e* before a suffix beginning with a consonant. Examples: *care + ful = careful, care + less = careless.* (An exception is *argue + ment = argument.*)

Note: Keep in mind that not all children learn effectively by the use of rules.

F.   Make lists of common prefixes and suffixes, as well as "families of sounds." (See Appendix G.)

G.   Teach them how to use the dictionary in locating unfamiliar words. Practice this usage on difficult words which can be found by the sounds of the first few letters. Discuss possible spellings for certain words and sounds. Also teach the use of the diacritical markings in the dictionary.

H.   Let the children exchange papers and "proofread" each others' written work. The habit of proofreading will carry over into their own writing.

I.   Let the children correct their own papers after taking a spelling test. Some children seem to be much more adept at correcting their own work than others. You will need to make periodic checks to determine whether the students are having difficulty finding and correcting their own errors.

27. Undeveloped Dictionary Skills

RECOGNIZED BY

Pupil is unable to locate words in a dictionary; use diacritical markings in determining the correct punctuation of words; or find the proper meaning for a word as used in a particular context.

DISCUSSION

In addition to the most common errors listed in the "Recognized By" section there are a number of other dictionary skills with which the student needs to become proficient in order to make the dictionary a really useful tool. The following list are other skills the students should learn.

> The use of guide words
> The use of accent
> The use of syllabication
> Interpreting phonetic respellings
> Using cross references
> Determining plurals
> Determining parts of speech
> Determining verb tense

The dictionary can be the most useful tool the child will ever possess for independent word analysis. Some students are able to become quite adept at using a dictionary in the second grade; however, most students learn in the third grade, and the skill should be learned no later than the fourth grade.

RECOMMENDATIONS

A. Follow the steps listed for teaching the dictionary procedure. Make sure the pupils are adept at each skill before beginning the next one.

   1. Make sure the child knows the sequence of the letters in the alphabet.

   2. Give several letters to be arranged alphabetically: *a, g, d, b, h,* and *m.*

3. Give several words which have different first letters to be arranged alphabetically: *bat, game, calf, dog,* and *man.*

4. Give several words which have the same beginning letters but different second letters to be arranged alphabetically: *pie, pliers, poker,* and *pack.*

5. Give several words which have the same beginning and second letters but different third letters: *pig, pie, pile,* and *picnic.*

B. Explain the purpose of the guide words at the top of the pages in a dictionary. Have the children write the beginning and ending guide words on pages that the words they are looking for are found.

C. Use words which are clearly defined by the context of the sentences. Have the children use the dictionary to find the proper meanings for the way in which the words were used in the sentences. Have them write the definitions and then use the words with the same meaning in a sentence.

D. Teach the use of diacritical markings. Almost all dictionaries contain a pronunciation key at the bottom of each page which serves as a guide for teaching this skill.

E. Give students two guide words printed at the top of a piece of paper. Then list a number of words and give students a short amount of time to tell whether the words listed would be found on the same page as the two guide words (five to seven seconds). Time them and have them place a plus (+) after each word that would come on the same page as *key* and *kick* and a minus (−) after each word that would not come on the same page. This assignment will enable students to learn to use guide words rapidly.

key	kick
keyway	+
kill	−
khan	+
kibe	+
kidney	−

F. Give students lists of words that they are not likely to be able to pronounce. Have them look up their phonetic respellings and write them beside each word. Have students then take turns reading the pronunciation of each word and let other students agree or disagree with each pronunciation.

G. Give students lists of words that have their accent in two places depending upon the part of speech in which they are used (such as *research*). Let students look the words up in their dictionaries and inductively decide where like words are usually accented as nouns and where they are usually accented as verbs. Other examples are *combat,* and *contract.*

GAMES AND EXERCISES

Today's Words

Purpose: To provide practice in the use of the dictionary and to increase vocabulary

Materials: A dictionary for each child

Procedure:

Each morning place three or four new words on the chalkboard. Use words that the children have not previously studied. Later in the day ask questions of the class which use the new words. For example, "Miguel, does *pollution* affect our city?"

Synonym Race

Purpose: To provide practice in using the dictionary to find synonyms. This assignment will increase the child's vocabulary and improve his comprehension in silent reading.

Materials: A basal reader
A dictionary for each student

Procedure:

You select sentences from the current reading lesson which include words which you wish the students to study. Write these sentences on the board, underlining the words for which the class is to look up synonyms. The pupils race to see who can supply the most synonyms from their dictionaries.

1.   The starfish does not *please* him.
    1.   satisfy   3.   attract
    2.   amuse   4.   gratify
2.   Water ran in a puddle all over his *clean* house.
    1.   pure   3.   unsoiled
    2.   spotless   4.   immaculate

Written Directions

Purpose: To provide practice in following directions and in the use of the dictionary

Materials: A dictionary for each student in the game
A set of cards or pieces of paper with directions written on them

Procedure:

Give each child a piece of paper on which there is a set of directions. Be sure that the directions are simple, but also include at least one new word which the child will need to find in the dictionary before he can follow his directions. As the children find the meanings of words they have looked up in the dictionary, they then can take turns pantomiming the action described by the directions. The other children try to guess what they are doing and try to guess the word or a synonym for it. If they guess a synonym for a new word, then both the word and the synonym may be written by each child. This practice will help the whole class to remember the meanings of new words. Some examples of directions for the game are as follows:

1. Pretend you are a vagabond.

2. Pretend you are wicked.

3. Pretend you have a halo.

Categories

Purpose: To provide practice on word meaning

Materials: Envelopes
             Cards with words on them that the children do not know well
             8½″ x 11″ paper or tagboard

Procedure:

At the top of a number of sheets of tagboard write three categories in which words may fall (see the following examples). Place these sheets of tagboard in manila envelopes along with approximately thirty words which will fit the categories listed. Pass the envelopes out to the children and have them use their dictionaries to group the words on the small word cards under the proper categories. Number the envelopes and have the children keep a list of the envelopes that they have done.

What animals do	Things that grow	Things that are not alive
fight	trees	rocks
run	cats	books
play	people	paper
jump	weeds	chalk
eat	frogs	chairs
sleep	elephants	pencils
walk	flowers	magnets

Matching Word Meanings

Purpose: To increase vocabulary through the use of the dictionary or thesaurus

Materials: A word sheet similar to the example given
A dictionary for each child

Word List

BENT	COARSE	BENEVOLENCE		OLD
goodness	stoop	helpfulness	waning	amiability
kind	philanthropy	senile	cambered	knobby
bias	hooked	charitable	inelegant	arch
vulgar	elder	unsmooth	look	rough
aged	rippling	bowlike	chunky	curved
elderly	choppy	geriatrics	turn	

Procedure:

Have the children place words from the word list under the capitalized word which would be the best category for them.

28. Inability to Locate Information

RECOGNIZED BY

Pupil is unable to locate information in encyclopedias, *Reader's Guide to Periodical Literature,* the card catalog of the library, the *World Almanac,* and other sources.

Pupil is unable to use cross references and parts of books such as the table of contents, index, and appendix.

DISCUSSION

It is almost a necessity for pupils in the intermediate grades and up to be able to use some of the sources of information listed previously; however, students often lack the skills needed to locate information. Even at the high school level many pupils are unfamiliar with the use of the index and table of contents in their own textbooks.

Teachers can locate the types of difficulties students are encountering by giving an informal test similar to the following:

Name the part of your textbook which tells the beginning page number of the chapter on atoms.

Where would you look in your textbook to locate the meaning of the word *negotiate?*

Where in your textbook would you find some reference to the subject of atomic reactors?

Find the name of the magazine which published the following article: "_____."

Explain how you would locate the following book in the library: _____

How would you locate something on the subject of whales in the following set of encyclopedias: _____

What city in the United States has the largest population?

What is the purpose of the appendix of a book?

RECOMMENDATIONS

A. Discuss with the students the types of information found in encyclopedias. Also give exercises in which the pupil is required to locate certain volumes and then certain pieces of information using the letter and/or word guides provided.

B. Teach the use of cross references. Ask the students to find information on certain subjects which are covered under several headings.

C. Explain the use of the library card catalog. (See Appendix D.)

D. Teach the pupils how to locate information in the *Reader's Guide to Periodical Literature*. Assign reports which require its use for finding a number of references on a certain subject.

E. Explain the use of the *World Almanac*. Give exercises in its use; for example, ask specific questions such as: "What city has the largest population in the world?" "What city covers the most square miles?"

F. Explain the use of the table of contents, index, and appendix. Do not take it for granted that older students know how to use these. Ask specific questions over their use: e.g., "What chapter explains the use of maps?" "What page contains an explanation of photosynthesis?" "Where would you find tables showing the relationships between weight and measures in the English and metric systems?"

GAMES AND EXERCISES

Student Travel Bureau

Purpose: To provide practice in research and map study skills

Materials: Globes
            Road maps
            Travel folders
            Various encyclopedias

Procedure:

When the pupils are studying a unit on map study, or any other time you desire, arrange the room as a travel bureau. Advertise the class's service much the same as a travel bureau would. If pupils bring in information concerning future trips their family will be taking, you can:

1. Present the traveler with a well-marked road map after studying maps from several companies and after corresponding with state highway departments

2. List places they may wish to visit along the way
3. Provide a history of landmarks along the way
4. Provide other specific information as called for

Thesaurus Puzzle

Purpose: To help children increase their vocabularies through the use of synonyms and antonyms

Materials: Pocket chart
             Word cards
             Envelopes

Procedure:

Divide the pocket chart into two columns. In the left-hand column, place a list of words which have synonyms or antonyms. Each child is given an envelope of word cards containing synonyms and antonyms of the word list. Each child then selects a word from his envelope which is either the synonym or antonym of one of the given words and places his word card on the right-hand side of the chart. A more advanced arrangement of this game can be made through the use of a thesaurus. Given a word in Column One, the children can use the thesaurus to make their own word cards for Column Two.

play	
white	
eager	
rare	
easy	
pleasant	
healthy	
cleanse	
guess	
clear	
dwarf	

List Completion
(For upper grades of junior high school only)

Purpose: To provide practice in the use of the thesaurus

Materials: A thesaurus
             The materials shown

Procedure:

Provide lists of words for the children to complete.

Directions: Complete the lists with words which mean almost the same thing.

1. decide	1. erratic	1. charge
2.	2.	2.
3.	3.	3.

1. deck	1. cage	1. charm
2.	2.	2.
3.	3.	3.

Detective

Purpose: To provide practice in locating information and skimming

Materials: Xerox copies of paragraphs from the basal reader, social studies, or science book the children are using. From one xeroxed copy you then can make a spirit master and make multiple copies of a certain paragraph if you desire.

Procedure:

Xerox a copy of a certain paragraph from a book that the child has in his desk. Make sure that the paragraph is about some particular bit of information that probably would be found in a certain book. Also you should use paragraphs which give a clue that can be found in the table of contents or in the index of the book. Tables and graphs are also appropriate if the book has a list of them. Put one of each of these paragraphs, graphs, or tables in an envelope along with a blank sheet of paper. Each child is given an envelope and the assignment to find where the paragraph came from by using the table of contents, index, list of tables and graphs, or appendix. When he finds the answer (when he finds the same paragraph in his textbook) he writes the information on the blank piece of paper and hands it back to you. Number the envelopes and have the child keep records of which envelopes he has done.

Appendix A

VOWEL SOUNDS

Short Sounds		Long Sounds	
a	bat	a	rake
e	bed	e	jeep
i	pig	i	kite
o	lock	o	rope
u	duck	u	mule

W is sometimes used as a vowel, as in the *ow* and *aw* teams. It is usually a vowel on word endings and a consonant at the beginning of words.

Y is usually a consonant when it appears at the beginning of a word, and a vowel in any other position.

Three consonants usually affect or control the sounds of some, or all, of the vowels when they follow these vowels within a syllable. They are: *r, w,* and *l.*

r (all vowels)	*w, (a, e,* and *o)*	*l (a)*
car	law	all
her	few	
dirt	now	
for		
fur		

CONSONANT SOUNDS

b	bear	*k*	king	*s*	six
c	cat	*l*	lake	*t*	turtle
d	dog	*m*	money	*v*	vase
f	face	*n*	nose	*w*	wagon
g	goat	*p*	pear	*x*	xylophone
h	hen	*q*	queen	*y*	yellow
j	jug	*r*	rat	*z*	zebra

The following consonants have two or more sounds:

c	cat	*g*	goat	*s*	six	*x*	*x*ylophone
c	i*c*e	*g*	germ	*s*	i*s*	*x*	e*x*ist
						x	bo*x*

When *g* is followed by *e, i,* or *y,* it usually takes the soft sound of *j,* as in *gentle* and *germ.* If it is not followed by these letters it takes the hard sound illustrated in such words as *got* and *game.*

When *c* is followed by *e, i,* or *y,* it usually takes the soft sound heard in *cent.* If it is not followed by these letters, it usually takes the hard sound heard in *come.*

Qu usually has the sound of *kw;* however, in some words such as *bouquet* it has the sound of *k.*

S sometimes takes a slightly different sound in words such as *sure.*

CONSONANT BLENDS

BEGINNING

bl	*bl*ue	*pr*	*pr*etty	*tw*	*tw*elve
br	*br*own	*sc*	*sc*ore	*wr*	*wr*ench
cl	*cl*own	*sk*	*sk*ill	*sch*	*sch*ool
cr	*cr*own	*sl*	*sl*ow	*scr*	*scr*een
dr	*dr*ess	*sm*	*sm*all	*shr*	*shr*ink
dw	*dw*ell	*sn*	*sn*ail	*spl*	*spl*ash
fl	*fl*ower	*sp*	*sp*in	*spr*	*spr*ing
fr	*fr*om	*st*	*st*ory	*squ*	*squ*ash
gl	*gl*ue	*sw*	*sw*an	*str*	*str*ing
gr	*gr*ape	*tr*	*tr*ee	*thr*	*thr*ow
pl	*pl*ate				

ENDING

nd	frie*nd*
*ng	bri*ng*
nk	i*nk*
nt	a*nt*
rk	wo*rk*
rt	hu*rt*
st	la*st*

* Sometimes considered to be a digraph.

DIGRAPHS

CONSONANT

ch	*ch*ute	*sh*	*sh*ip
ch	*ch*oral	*th*	*th*ree
ch	*ch*urch	*th*	*th*at
gh	cou*gh*	*wh*	*wh*ich
ph	gra*ph*	*wh*	*wh*o

VOWEL (MOST COMMON PHONEMES ONLY)

ai	p*ai*n	*ie*	p*ie*ce	*ow*	l*ow*
ay	h*ay*	(A number of other		*ue*	tr*ue*
ea	*ea*ch	phonemes are common)		*ui*	b*ui*ld
or		*oa*	*oa*ts	or	
ea	w*ea*ther	*oe*	f*oe*	*ui*	fr*ui*t
ee	tr*ee*	*oo*	b*oo*k		
ei	w*ei*ght	*oo*	b*oo*t		
or		*ou*	t*ou*gh (May be either a diagraph		
ei	*ei*ther		or a diphthong)		

DIPHTHONGS*

au	h*au*l	*oi*	s*oi*l
aw	h*aw*k	*ou*	tr*ou*t
ew	f*ew*	*ow*	c*ow*
ey	th*ey*	*oy*	b*oy*

_____

* In saying a diphthong sound one must change the position of the mouth. In saying a digraph sound this is not necessary.

Appendix B

SOURCES OF READING MATERIALS

Games

Games are worthwhile for improving abilities in blends, consonants, vowels, and digraphs; diphthongs and sight word tests are useful to examine basic sight words.

Barnell-Loft, Ltd., and
Dexter and Westbrook, Ltd.
958 Church St.
Baldwin, NY 11510

Educational Games Center
2797 South 450 West
Bountiful, UT 84010

Garrard Publishing
1607 N. Market St.
Champaign, IL 61820

Ideal School Supply
11000 S. Lavergne Ave.
Oak Lawn, IL 60453

Kenworthy Educational Service
138 Allen St.
Buffalo, NY 14205

Lyons and Carnahan
Educational Publishers
407 East 25th St.
Chicago, IL 60616

Science Research Associates
259 East Erie St.
Chicago, IL 60611

High Interest—Low Vocabulary Books

There are many new books which are reportedly high interest—low vocabulary materials. Some of these, however, are not appealing to children. Following is a helpful list of the better books.

BENEFIC PRESS
10300 W. Roosevelt Rd.
Westchester, IL 60153

Animal Adventure Series. A series of twelve books written at the primer to first grade level, with interest levels that tend to run one to three grades above their reading grade level.

Butternut Bill Series. A series of eight books written at the preprimer to first grade reading level with interest levels that tend to run from one to three grades above their reading grade level.

Button Family Adventure Series.   A series of twelve books written at the preprimer to third grade level with interest levels that tend to run about two grades above their reading grade level.

Cowboy Sam Series.   A series of fifteen books with reading levels ranging from preprimer to third grade. Their interest levels tend to run to two to three grades above their reading grade level.

Dan Frontier Series.   A series of eleven books with reading levels ranging from preprimer to fourth grade. Their interest levels tend to run to two to three grades above their reading level.

Inner City Series.   A series of five books written at the second to fourth grade reading level with interest levels that tend to run from two to three grades above their reading grade level.

Mystery Adventure Series.   A series of six books written at the second to sixth grade level. These mystery stories about teen-age boys and girls have interest levels two to ten grades above their reading grade level.

Racing Wheels Series.   A series of six books written at the second to fourth grade level with interest levels that tend to run from two to eight grades above their reading grade level.

Salior Jack Series.   A series of ten books written at the preprimer to third grade reading level with interest levels that tend to run two to three grades above their reading grade level.

Space Age Books.   A series of eight books written at the preprimer to third grade reading level with interest levels that tend to run from one to three grades above their reading level.

Sports Mystery Series.   These are stories about teen-agers, their problems, and sports activities. It is a series of eight books written at the second to fourth grade level with interest levels that tend to run from two to eight grades above their reading grade level.

Target Today Series.   A series of four books written at the second to sixth grade levels. Each book contains many short stories dealing with life today. Various ethnic groups are represented. Interest levels tend to run from two to eight grades above their reading grade level.

D. C. HEATH AND COMPANY
125 Spring St.
Lexington, MA 02173

Teen-Age Tales.   A series of nine books written for teen-agers with reading problems. Their reading levels run from third through sixth grade with interest levels that tend to run from four to nine grades above their reading grade level.

Tom Logan Series.   A series of ten books written at the preprimer to third grade reading levels with interest levels that tend to run two to eight or nine grades above their reading grade level.

FIELD EDUCATIONAL PUBLICATIONS
2400 Hanover St.
Palto Alto, CA 94304

Deep Sea Adventure Series. A series of thirteen books written at the 1.8 to 5.0 reading levels with interest levels that tend to run two to eight or nine grades above their reading grade level.

GARRARD PUBLISHING
1607 N. Market St.
Champaign, IL 61820

First Reading Books. A series of sixteen books written at first grade level. Their interest level tends to run two to four grades above their reading level.

The Basic Vocabulary Series. This is a series of eight books with true-life and folklore stories from all over the world. Their reading level is about grade two and their interest level runs from grades one to six.

Pleasure Reading Books. This is a series of seven classic books that have been rewritten using a more simple vocabulary than the original editions. The reading level of these books is about grade four and the interest level ranges from grade three up.

RANDOM HOUSE
School Division
201 E. 50th St.
New York, NY 10022

Beginner Books. These are a series of about twenty-seven books written at the 2.1 to 2.5 grade levels. Many are well known as Dr. Seuss books. The interest levels range from grade one up.

Materials for Phonics Work

WEBSTER DIVISION, McGRAW-HILL
8171 Redwood Highway
Novato, CA 94947

Webster Word Wheels

CHARLES E. MERRILL PUBLISHING
1300 Alum Creek Dr.
Columbus, OH 43216

Merrill Phonics Skilltext Series

PHONOVISUAL PRODUCTS
P.O. Box 5625
Washington, D.C. 20016

Phonics Charts

HARCOURT BRACE JOVANOVICH
School Department
757 Third Ave.
New York, NY 10017
Speech-to-Print Phonics

Phonics Materials Which Individualize Instruction (also for basic sight words)

PSYCHOTECHNICS
1900 Pickwick Ave.
Glenview, IL 60025
Rx Reading Program

Phonics Structural Analysis Tests (Word Analysis Skills)

PSYCHOTECHNICS
1900 Pickwick Ave.
Glenview, IL 60025
Corrective Reading System

ALLYN AND BACON, LONGWOOD DIVISION
470 Atlantic Ave.
Boston, MA 02210
El Paso Phonics Survey. From *A Teacher's Handbook for Diagnosis and Remediation,* Ekwall.

ALLYN AND BACON
470 Atlantic Ave.
Boston, MA 02210
Ekwall Phonics Survey. From *Diagnosis and Remediation of the Disabled Reader,* Ekwall.

Books about Phonics

Burmeister, Lou E. *Words: From Print to Meaning.* Reading, Mass.: Addison-Wesley, 1975.

Ekwall, Eldon E. *A Teacher's Handbook for Diagnosis and Remediation.* Boston: Allyn and Bacon, 1977.

Trela, Thaddeus M. *Sensible Phonics.* Belmont, Calif.: Fearon, 1975.

Skill Development

BARNELL-LOFT, LTD.
958 Church St.
Baldwin, NY 11510
Specific Skill Series

Vocabulary, Structural and Phonetic Analysis

BELL AND HOWELL
7100 McCormick Rd.
Chicago, IL 60645
Language Master

Vocabulary, Word Analysis, Comprehension and Study Skills

CHARLES E. MERRILL
1300 Alum Creek Dr.
Columbus, OH 43216
Merrill Reading Skilltext Series

Comprehension, Vocabulary, and Study Skills

READERS DIGEST SERVICE
Educational Division
Pleasantville, NY 10570
New Advanced Reading Skill Builder

Vocabulary Development

BARNELL-LOFT, LTD.
958 Church St.
Baldwin, NY 11510
Picto-Cabulary Series

Vocabulary and Oral Reading Skills

HARCOURT BRACE JOVANOVICH
757 Third Ave.
New York, NY 10017
Plays for Echo Reading

Vocabulary Development, Word Analysis Skills, and Comprehension Skills

PSYCHOTECHNICS
1900 Pickwick Ave.
Glenview, IL 60025

Psychotechnics Radio Reading and *Vx Vocabulary Program*

Comprehension Skills

SCIENCE RESEARCH ASSOCIATES
259 East Erie Street
Chicago, IL 60611

SRA Pilot Libraries

Appendix C

ILLUSTRATING WORDS PER MINUTE PERCENT OF COMPREHENSION

Comprehension

PERCENT OF COMPREHENSION

100 90 80 70 60 50 40 30 20 10

Trials

1 2 3 4 5 6 7 8 9 10 11 12

Speed

WORDS PER MINUTE

1200 1100 1000 900 800 700 600 500 400 300 200 100

Trials

1 2 3 4 5 6 7 8 9 10 11 12

Appendix D

AUTHOR CARD

Call no.	395 G
Author	**Gray, Sheila J.**
Title	Blondes prefer gentlemen; redheads too—
Publisher & date of publication	brunettes included! Illus. by Bill Charmetz, Morrow, 1966.
Total number of pages in book	260p. illus.
Indicates subject heading in library card catalog Indicates there is a title card in card catalog	1. Etiquette 1. Title

TITLE CARD

	395 G
Title	Blondes Prefer Gentlement
Author Title	Gray, Sheila J. Blondes Prefer Gentlemen: redheads too— brunettes included! Illus. by Bill Charmetz. Morrow, 1966. 260p. illus. 1. Etiquette I. Title

SUBJECT CARD

395	
G	
Subject	Etiquette

Gray, Sheila J.
  Blondes Prefer Gentlemen: redheads too—
brunettes included! Illus. by Bill
Charmetz. Morrow, 1966.
    260p. illus.

  1. Etiquette   I. Title

  64

Subject

Author
Title

Appendix E

CODE FOR MARKING IN ORAL DIAGNOSIS

1. Circle all omissions.

2. Insert with a caret (⌒) all insertions

3. Draw a line through words for which substitutions or mispronunciations were made and write the substitution or mispronunciation over the word. Determine later whether the word missed was a substitution or mispronunciation.

4. If the student reads too fast to write in all mispronunciations, you may draw a line through the word and write a *P* over the word for partial mispronunciation or a *G* over the word for gross mispronunciation.

5. Use a dotted or wavy line to indicate repetitions.

6. Mark inversions in the same way as substitutions and later determine whether the mistake was really an inversion or a substitution.

7. Use an arched line to connect words where the student disregarded punctuation. (See line connecting *fair* and *he* in the paragraph example.)

8. Use brackets [   ] to enclose the words for which the pupil needed help.

9. Make a check (✔) over words that were self-corrected.

10. Make two vertical lines (‖) preceding a word where a pause appeared.

Tom drove his automobile to the county fair. He saw no place to park. He drove up and down between the rows of cars. Finally he decided to go home.

Appendix F

PREPOSITIONAL PHRASES

The following are commonly used phrases. Most of the words are also in the Fry list* of the 600 most frequently used words in reading and writing the English language.

about
about his dog
about my cat
about dinner
about my sister
about the room

along
along the ground
along the water
along the wall
along the road
along the way

as
as a house
as a girl
as a boy
as a man
as a woman

before
before winter
before bed
before the fire
before eight
before we go

by
by the hair
by the horse
by the week
by the government
by her eyes

after
after we've gone
after three years
after work
after his mother
after the bell

around
around the garden
around the school
around here
around eight o'clock
around the trees

at
at the house
at the door
at the party
at the water
at the half

but
but the outside
but the poor
but the yard
but his head
but her eyes

down
down the hill
down the side
down the front
down the street
down the stairs

---

* Edward Fry, *Reading Instruction for Classroom and Clinic* (New York: McGraw-Hill, 1972), pp. 58–63.

for
for the law
for the doctor
for the money
for a guess
for tomorrow

in
in the hour
in the music
in the spring
in the picture
in his voice

like
like the wind
like snow
like you
like her hat
like a bird

next
next turn
next president
next to me
next to him
next in line

off
off the wall
off the water
off the horse
off the table
off of it

out
out of paper
out to study
out of school
out of line
out in public

over
over his clothes
over the ice
over the city
over the thing
over his name

through
through them
through his heart
through twenty
through the day
through the water

from
from the cows
from her need
from my cousin
from the cold
from the story

into
into the box
into the floor
into the train
into the bank
into the office

near
near the fish
near the war
near the bridge
near the farm
near the airplane

of
of the sun
of my life
of the farm
of the paper
of the church

on
on one afternoon
on Friday morning
on her smile
on the house
on her face

outside
outside the country
outside the woods
outside the town
outside the third grade
outside the grocery store

to
to the summer
to the fair
to the state
to the world
to the house

up
up the window
up the river
up the table
up in the air
up to speak

until
until the night
until they come
until tomorrow
until this minute
until he knew

with
with his suit
with my uncle
with her aunt
with a present
with the baby

Appendix G

SUFFIXES

Suffix	Meaning	Examples	Used to Form
able (ible, ble)	able to, worthy of	obtainable divisible breakable	adjectives
ac (ic, al, an)	characteristic of, having to do with, caused by	cardiac alcoholic comical American	adjectives
aceous (acious)	characterized by, like	carbonaceous crustaecous tenacious	adjectives
ade	action, product	blockade limeade lemonade	nouns
age	act of, cost of	tillage passage postage	nouns
al	relating to, of, pertaining to	directional fictional dismissal	adjectives
al	action process	rehearsal arrival acquittal	nouns
an (ian, ean)	pertaining to, of, born in	diocesan Christian European	adjectives
an	one who, belonging to	artisan African American	nouns
ance (ence)	act of, state of being	continuance reference performance	nouns

Suffix	*Meaning*	*Examples*	*Used to Form*
ancy (ency)	state of being, act	efficiency piquancy emergency	nouns
ant (ent)	one who	accountant suppliant superintendent	nouns
ant	performing, promoting	litigant expectorant expectant	adjectives
ar	relating to, like, of the nature of	regular polar singular	adjectives
ard (art)	one who (excessively)	braggart dullard pollard	nouns
arium	place relating to	planetarium sanitarium aquarium	nouns
ary (ar)	relating to	military dictionary scholar	nouns
ate	office, function	directorate vicarate magistrate	nouns
ate	acted on	temperate determinate animate	adjectives
ate	to become, combine, arrange for	evaporate chlorinate orchestrate	verbs
ation (ition)	state of	translation realization nutrition	nouns
cle	little, small	article particle corpuscle	nouns
dom	state of being	wisdom martyrdom freedom	nouns

Suffix	Meaning	Examples	Used to Form
ed	tending to, having	cultured versed bigoted	adjectives
en	cause to have, made of	strengthen woolen wooden	nouns
en	to make, made of	deepen strengthen fasten	verbs
ent (ence)	quality, act, degree	solvent emergence despondence	nouns
er (ar, ior, yer)	a thing or action, connected with, or associated	batter beggar interior lawyer	nouns
ery (erie)	place to or for collection of	nunnery jewelry tanneries	nouns
esce	to begin	effervesce fluoresce coalesce	verbs
escent	starting to be	obsolescent fluorescent alkalescent	adjectives
esque	like, having quality or style of	picturesque Romanesque statuesque	adjectives
ess	female	patroness giantess princess	nouns
et (ette)	little, female	dinette suffragette pullet	nouns
ful	full of	hopeful playful joyful	adjectives

Suffix	*Meaning*	*Examples*	*Used to Form*
fy	to make, become	liquefy purify glorify	verbs
hood	state of, condition	womanhood childhood priesthood	nouns
eer	one who, calling or profession	auctioneer buccaneer profiteer	nouns
ic (ics)	relating to, affected with	alcoholic allergic volcanic	adjectives
ic (ical)	one that produces	magic cosmetic radical	nouns
ice	condition or quality of	malice justice practice	nouns
ie	small, little	doggie lassie	nouns
ile (il)	appropriate to, suited for, capable of	docile missile civil	adjectives
ing	related to, made of	farthing banking cooking	nouns
ion (sion)	result of act, state	regulation hydration correction	nouns
ise (ize)	to make, treat with	sterilize summarize finalize	verbs
ish	having	boyish purplish fortyish	adjectives
ism	act of, state of	baptism invalidism animalism	nouns

Suffix	*Meaning*	*Examples*	*Used to Form*
ist	practicer or believer in one who, the doer	evangelist pianist violinist	nouns
ive	related to, tending to	creative massive amusive	adjectives
ize	to become, become like	Americanize crystallize socialize	verbs
kin	little	catkin manikin napkin	nouns
le (el)	small, a thing used for for doing	icicle handle mantle	nouns
less	without, lacking	careless hopeless painless	adjectives
ling	young, small	duckling hireling suckling	nouns
ly	in a way, manner	softly quietly hoarsely	adverbs
ment	concrete result, state, process	embankment development amazement	nouns
ness	state of being	happiness cheerfulness hopelessness	nouns
ock	small one	hillock bullock paddock	nouns
or	state of, does certain thing	pallor grantor elevator	nouns
orium	place for, giving	sanatorium auditorium haustorium	nouns

Suffix	Meaning	Examples	Used to Form
ory	tending to, producing	auditory gustatory justificatory	adjectives
ose	full of, containing, like	verbose cymose morose	adjectives
ous	having, full of	religious generous poisonous	adjectives
ship	state of, office, art	friendship clerkship horsemanship	nouns
ster	one that does or is	spinster teamster youngster	nouns
th	act of, state of	growth length spilth	nouns
tude	condition	certitude gratitude finitude	nouns
ty (ity)	state of, degree, quality	masculinity priority timidity	nouns
ulent	tending to, abounds in	fraudulent flocculent opulent	adjectives
ure	act, office	exposure legislature procedure	nouns
ward	in specified direction	southward seaward backward	adverbs
wise	manner, way	likewise clockwise lengthwise	adverbs
y	like a, full of	rosy fishy glassy	adjectives

Suffix	Meaning	Examples	Used to Form
y (acy)	state of, action, condition, position	jealousy inquiry celibacy	nouns

PREFIXES

Prefix	Meaning	Examples
a	on, in, at	alive asleep abed
a (an)	not, without	anhydrous anhydride anarchy
*ab, abs	from	abduct abrogate abstain
*ad (ac, af, ag, al, an, ap, ar, as, at)	*to,* at, toward	adapt accuse aggrade acclaim affirm
ambi (amb)	both	ambicoloration ambivalent ambidextrous
amphi (amph)	both, around	amphibian amphitheatre amphibolite
ana	back, again up, similar to	analysis analogy anabaptist
ante	before, earlier date	antechamber antedate antetype
anti (ant, anth)	against, counteracts, prevents	antilabor antiaircraft antitoxin
apo (ap)	off, away from, used before	apology aphelion apocrine

Prefix	Meaning	Examples
archi (arch)	chief, extreme	architect archenemy archfiend
auto	self-propelling self	automobile autotruck autobiography
*be	to make, about, *by*	belittle beguile befriend
bene	well	benefit benefactor benevolent
bi	having two, double	bicycle bilingual byweekly
by	near, extra	bystander by-pass by-product
cata (cat, cath)	down, against	catastrophic catacomb catheter
centi	one hundred	centigrade centimeter centipede
circum	around, about	circumnavigate circumpolar circumspect
com (co, col, con, cor)	*with,* together, intensification	combine copilot collect confided corrupt
contra	against	contradict contraband contrarious
counter	opposite, in retaliation, opposed to but like	counterclockwise counterattack counterpart

Prefix	Meaning	Examples
*de	from, away	deport detract devitalize
deca (dec, deka, dek)	ten	decimal decade decagon
di (dis)	twice, double	disect dichroism dichloride
dia	through, across	diagonal diagram diagnose
*dis	opposite, refuse to, *apart*	disagree disintegrate disable disengage
ec (ex)	out of, from	eccentric exodus exaggerate
*en	in, into make	encircle enact encourage
enter	to go into, among	enterprise entered entertain
epi (ep)	upon, after, over	epitaph epilogue epicene
equi	equal	equilibrium equilateral equiangular
*ex	out	exile exhale exhaust
eu	well	euphony euphonism eugenic

Prefix	Meaning	Examples
extra	beyond	extraordinary extrajudicial extracurricular
for	very, neglect, away	forlorn forbid forget
fore	before, in front	forepaws forehand foreleg
geo	earth, ground, soil	geography geographic geology
hemi	half	hemisphere hemicycle hemistich
hexa (hex)	six	hexagon hexapod hexachord
hyper	over, above	hypersensitive hyperactive hyperacid
hypo	under, beneath	hypocrite hypocycloid hypodermic
*in (il, im, ir)	in, within, *into*	inbreed instigate infect
*in (il, im, ir)	no, *not,* without	illiterate immaterial insignificant irresponsible
inter	between, with	interurban interlock interact
intra	within, inside of	intrastate intravenous intramural

Prefix	*Meaning*	*Examples*
intro	into, within	introvert introspective introduce
kilo	one thousand	kilowatt kilogram kilocycle
mal (male)	bad, wrong, ill	maladjust malediction maladroit
meta (met)	after, change in place or form	metacarpal metabolism metaprotein
milli	one thousand	milligram millimeter milliard
mis (miso)	wrong	misplace misadventure misanthrope
mono (mon)	one	monosyllable monologue monolayer
multi	many	multitude multiply multiphase
non	not	nonunion nondemocratic nonzero
ob (oc, of, op)	to, upon, totally	object occur offer oppose
oct, (octa, octo)	eight	October octagon octopod
off	from	offspring offset offstage

Prefix	Meaning	Examples
out	beyond, excels	outtalk outweigh outmaneuver
over	too much	overactive overheated overage
par (para)	by, past, accessory	parallel paragraph parasympathetic
penta (pent)	five	pentagon Pentateuch pentane
per	through, completely	perceive persuade perchloride
peri	around, about	perimeter periphery periscope
phono (phon, phone)	voice, sound	phonograph phonate phoneme
poly	many	polygon polygamy polysulfide
post	later, behind	postgraduate postaxial postlude
*pre	*before,* in front (of), superior	prewar preaxial pre-eminent
*pro	moving forward, acting for, defending, favoring, *in front of*	progress pronoun prosecutor prolabor prologue
quadr	four	quadrant quadrangle quadrennial

Prefix	Meaning	Examples
quint	five	quintuplets quintet quintillion
*re (red)	*back,* again	review regain recall
retro	backwards,	retroactive retrospect retroflex
semi	half, partly, twice in (period)	semicircle semicivilized semiannually
sex (sexi)	six	sextant sexpartite sexivalent
*sub (suc, suf, sug, sup, sur, sus)	*under*	submarine succeed suffix
super	above, exceeding	superior superstructure superscribe
sur	over, above, beyond	surcoat surface surbase
syn (sym)	with, together	sympathy synthesis symptom
tele (tel)	afar, of, in, or by	television telescope telephoto
trans	across	transcontinental transport transatlantic
tri	three	triangle tricycle triweekly
ultra	beyond, excessively	ultraviolet ultramodern ultramarine

Prefix	Meaning	Examples
*un	*not,* opposite	unannounced unburden uncrowned
uni	consisting of only one	unicellular uniform unicorn
under	below	underpaid underworked underpass
vice	in place of	viceroy vice-president vice-consul
with	against, away	withstand withdraw withhold

---

*Prefixes which appeared most frequently and accounted for 82 percent of the 61 different basic forms of prefixes studied by Stauffer. The italicized word represents the meaning of the prefix in the study referred to here. From Russell G. Stauffer, *Teaching Reading as a Thinking Process* (New York: Harper & Row, 1969), p. 348.

Appendix H

BASIC SIGHT WORDS*

Should be known by†			Words			
1.9	a	him	then	time	find	red
	did	look	who	after	is	that
	have	run	can	came	other	way
	know	we	good	he	something	blue
	one	be	in	now	very	give
	to	for	not	she	around	may
	and	his	this	tree	fly	ride
	do	make	will	all	jump	them
	her	said	come	could	over	went
	like	what	has	help	stop	by
	play	big	it	old	want	green
	too	get	of	so	as	me
	are	house	three	up	from	sat
	down	my	you	am	let	there
	here	the	your	day	ran	when
	little	where	about	how	take	saw
	put	but	call	on	was	they
	two	go	had	some	back	would
	away	I	mother	us	funny	yes
	eat	no	see	an	man	
2.5	again	well	stand	please	morning	happy
	dog	been	yellow	think	under	walk
	boy	any	were	tell	party	much
	if	far	before	better	black	fun
	brown	ask	white	than	pretty	must
	into	fast	five	four	long	girl
	buy	at	why	thank	pull	name
	just	laugh	light	or	Mr.	got
	cold	ate	with	their	rabbit	never
	new	night	soon	out	more	high
	color	ball	work	these	read	shall
	sleep	walk				

* Eldon E. Ekwall, *Corrective Reading System* "Basic Sight Words," (Glenview, Illinois: Psychotechnics, 1976).

† The designation 1.9 means the word should be known by the ninth month of the first grade; 2.5 means it should be known by the fifth month of the second grade, etc.

Should be known by			*Words*			
2.9	always	another	because	best	both	box
	bring	carry	clean	cut	does	each
	end	every	fall	first	found	friend
	gave	full	left	own	start	year
	last	our	six	wish	kind	open
	sit	while	keep	only	show	which
	hurt	once	should	warm	hot	men
	near	school	until	home	say	those
	hold	many	round	thing	hand	made
	right	ten	grow	live	pick	sure
3.5	dear	drink	present	seem	sing	such
	today	use	write	done	people	seven
	small	try	wash			
3.9	draw	eight	upon	leave	its	goes

Index

Affix
definition of, 3
list of. (*See* Appendix G, 151)

Basal reader, definition of, 3
Basic sight words
definition of, 3
games and exercises for remediation
of difficulty with, 31–38
list of. (*See* Appendix H, 165)
possible causes of difficulty with, 29
recognition of difficulty with, 29
recommendations for remediation
for difficulty with, 30–31
Blends
definition of, 3
list of. (*See* Appendix A, 136)
recommendations for remediation of
difficulty with, 73–74
testing for knowledge of, 73

Card files, for learning new words, 40
Choral reading, definition of, 3
Code for marking in oral diagnosis,
147
Comprehension
commonly listed subskills, 88–89
games and exercises for remediation
of difficulty with, 95–107
recognizing difficulty with, 88
recommendations for remediation of
difficulty with, 89–95
Consonants
games and exercises for remediation
of difficulty with, 58–66
list of. (*See* Appendix A, 135)
recommendations for remediation of
difficulty with, 57–58
testing for knowledge of, 57

Context clues
recognizing difficulty with, 82
recommendations for inability to
use, 82–84
Contractions
list of, 85–86
recognition of difficulty with, 85
recommendations for remediation of
difficulty with, 86–87
testing for knowledge of, 85
corrective reading, definition of, 4
CRS (Corrective Reading System), 57
source of. (*See* Appendix B, 141)

Developmental reading, definition of, 4
Diagnosis, definition of, 3
Dictionary skills
games and exercises for improving,
128–30
list of, 126
recognizing difficulty with, 126
recommendations for remediation of
difficulty with, 126–27
Digraph
definition of, 3
list of. (*See* Appendix A, 137)
recommendations for remediation of
difficulty with, 73–74
testing for knowledge of, 73
Diphthong
definition of, 3
list of. (*See* Appendix A, 137)
recommendations for remediation of
difficulty with, 73–74
testing for knowledge of, 73

Ekwall Phonics Survey, source of. (*See*
Appendix B, 141)